"Jason Gaboury has written a master[...] loneliness. He takes us on a journey [...] native. From Genesis to the Gospels, Jason describes loneliness as a human condition God uses for our transformation and his transcendent purposes in us. This is an invitation into the ultimate antidote for loneliness—communion with God and biblical community."

Mac Pier, founder of Movement.org, Lausanne catalyst for cities

"In these pages, you won't find an easy solution to the 'problem' of loneliness. What *Wait with Me* offers instead is far wiser and more daring: an invitation into deeper life with the God who eagerly inhabits our isolation and lingers with us there. For anyone who knows firsthand the slow-bleeding pain of loneliness, this honest and hopeful and paradigm-bending book is worth pondering, worth lingering on."

Gregory Coles, author of *Single, Gay, Christian*

"This, thankfully, is not a book that promises to solve loneliness. It's not a how-to guide for 'getting out there' or a formula for ensuring God will erase your sense of isolation. This book is something very different: a poignant, wise, at times searing invitation to attend to our loneliness as a call from God. This is spiritual writing that is at once urgent and patient, honest and inviting."

James K. A. Smith, Byker Chair in Applied Reformed Theology and Worldview at Calvin University, author of *On the Road with Saint Augustine*

"We're lonelier than ever, and we don't like it. Instead of avoiding or escaping this all-too-human condition, this book honestly and refreshingly invites us to stay with it and find Jesus in the spaces and places where we'd rather not be. Read and find healing for your soul."

James Choung, vice president of strategy and innovation for InterVarsity/USA, author of *True Story* and *Longing for Revival*

"Jason and his wife, Sophia, have been mentors to my wife and me for several years. Their depth of wisdom in marriage, parenting, and faith is remarkable. They have shared many life-shifting words with us over delicious meals in tiny NYC apartments."

Andy Mineo, hip-hop recording artist

"Like an adept theater director, Jason Gaboury weaves together the fallibilities and surprising strengths of biblical characters into a compelling performance that leaves readers astonished to discover they are staring into the face of their own hidden stories. Reading this book is like having a companion on life's journey who knows the pain of isolation but whose gentle presence creates spaces for discovering new possibilities for spiritual development and emotional maturity. For anyone who has ever felt lonely, this eloquent book is a must-read."

Sarah Dunlop, lecturer in practical theology, Ridley Hall, Cambridge, UK

"It is not easy to find biblical, relevant, practical, and emotionally engaged content that presses us into the tension of existence as opposed to showing us how to manage or get away. This book is not a roadmap on how to escape something that is core to being human but a testament to how rigorous engagement with loneliness can free us to live more fully as people made in the image of God. This isn't just a book you should buy; it is a book you should read."

Jonathan P. Walton, poet and author of *Twelve Lies That Hold America Captive: And the Truth That Sets Us Free*

"Jason Gaboury's witness to the disturbingly universal experience of loneliness cuts right to the heart of what it means to be human—what it means to enter this unwelcomed, unavoidable, yet potentially sacred meeting place. He guides us to consider loneliness as a fount from which spiritual intimacy flows as we exchange empathy with God, both offering and receiving from the other. Readers will be drawn into authentic prayer and reflection, and then gently sent back into a world drowning in the confusion of loneliness with new vision for the possibilities of this strange phenomenon's dark gifts."

David L. Booram, cofounder and director of Fall Creek Abbey, coauthor of *When Faith Becomes Sight*

"At first glance, loneliness and solitude look a lot alike. But upon a closer examination, loneliness is mostly just alone, and solitude, as a spiritual practice, is alone *with God*. That makes all the difference. In *Wait with Me*, Jason helps us see how our own places of loneliness could became places of solitude in the Presence. I love the way his writing is so well-rooted in Scripture stories."

Alan Fadling, founder and president of Unhurried Living, coauthor of *What Does Your Soul Love?*

"Jason Gaboury knows the ache of loneliness from the inside and agrees with God's assessment of his good creation: it is not good for us to be alone. But what if loneliness can enlarge not only our compassion and empathy for others but also our devotion and love for Christ? What if loneliness becomes an opportunity not only to know God's presence in our affliction but to know Jesus in his? With skillful exposition of Scripture and an undaunted naming of pain, Gaboury invites us into a paradigm shift that is both hope filled and liberating."

Sharon Garlough Brown, author of the Sensible Shoes Series and *Shades of Light*

"*Wait with Me* reads as a devotional gently inviting the audience into a posture of vulnerable connection with Christ. Jason imaginatively weaves deeply moving personal narrative with Scripture in a way that brings biblical truths about God's presence to life. At various points I found myself needing to stop and ponder my way forward with Jesus. I highly recommend this book for anyone who desires to meet Jesus in their loneliness or who seeks to understand those of us who often long for more."

Noemi Vega Quiñones, coauthor of *Hermanas*, area ministry director with InterVarsity Christian Fellowship

Wait With

Me

MEETING GOD
IN LONELINESS

JASON GABOURY

An imprint of InterVarsity Press
Downers Grove, Illinois

InterVarsity Press
P.O. Box 1400, Downers Grove, IL 60515-1426
ivpress.com
email@ivpress.com

InterVarsity Press® is the book-publishing division of InterVarsity Christian Fellowship/USA®, a movement of students and faculty active on campus at hundreds of universities, colleges, and schools of nursing in the United States of America, and a member movement of the International Fellowship of Evangelical Students. For information about local and regional activities, visit intervarsity.org.

Scripture quotations, unless otherwise noted, are from the New Revised Standard Version of the Bible, copyright 1989 by the Division of Christian Education of the National Council of the Churches of Christ in the USA. Used by permission. All rights reserved.

While any stories in this book are true, some names and identifying information may have been changed to protect the privacy of individuals.

Cover design and image composite: David Fassett
Interior design: Daniel van Loon

ISBN 978-0-8308-4668-9 (print)
ISBN 978-0-8308-4388-6 (digital)

Printed in the United States of America ♾

InterVarsity Press is committed to ecological stewardship and to the conservation of natural resources in all our operations. This book was printed using sustainably sourced paper.

Library of Congress Cataloging-in-Publication Data
A catalog record for this book is available from the Library of Congress.

P   25 24 23 22 21 20 19 18 17 16 15 14 13 12 11 10 9 8 7 6 5 4 3 2 1

Y   38 37 36 35 34 33 32 31 30 29 28 27 26 25 24 23 22 21 20

To Sophia,
whose partnership in life
and ministry exceeds my greatest hope.

To Malaya and Serena,
who tuned my heart to discover my life
with God in daily rhythms of work and play.

Contents

1 | See

"**To** be human is to be lonely," Friar Ugo said to me, his voice cracking with age.

For forty years he served as a Jesuit missionary on the African continent. Now he was sitting across from me, a thirty-something campus minister trying to make sense of God and my deep loneliness. Despite the gentleness, even fragility, of his appearance, Friar Ugo's words pierced the space between us like a spiritual searchlight.

My heartbeat sounded in my ears, and I pressed my lips together waiting, *Say something else*, I thought. *Anything.*

I've wrestled with loneliness ever since I can remember, perhaps before I can remember. Growing up, my mother would tell stories about our separation at the hospital during the first six weeks of my life, or about times when, as a baby, I'd cry inconsolably for hours. Exasperated, Mom got in the habit of turning up the stereo and leaving me to cry it out. I don't know what impact either of these situations had on my emerging sense of connection, but I can remember feeling lonely.

That sense of loneliness dogged me through childhood, college, and into adulthood. If Friar Ugo had observed my life from the outside, *lonely* would not be the adjective quick to mind. With two girls in elementary school, our home was filled with Play-Doh, colored paper, and playdates. Sophia and I parented together and partnered in ministry. Our home was often full of students, friends from church, and neighbors from our building. I even had a reputation in our church for being an expert on building community.

Still, loneliness persisted. Washing dishes late on a Tuesday night after a group of friends had gone home, I'd feel strangely lonely, isolated, unknown, and unloved. Clearly, something wasn't working. *If anyone could help me*, I thought, *Friar Ugo could*. I made an appointment to talk to him, determined to resolve this sense of isolation.

For twenty minutes I'd talked about the ache of loneliness I felt even though it didn't make sense. Ugo didn't interrupt. He sat still as the furniture, his eyes dancing with something I couldn't place: insight, amusement, wisdom?

That conversation would change my life.

"Loneliness is all around us," Friar Ugo said. Of course, I knew that. Why else would I be sitting in this chair across from this old friar? You know it too. Perhaps you've picked up this book because you know the ache of loneliness in your situation. A friend who lived alone for many years said, "The hardest thing for me was just coming home and not having anyone to ask, 'How was your day?'" Perhaps it seems as if all the friends you used to talk with into the early morning hours have moved away or gotten married. Perhaps you're a young parent caught in the valley of diapers, isolated from other adults, and emotionally exhausted. Perhaps you're in a new job or school and miss the familiar faces and relationships.

The technological solution to our loneliness seems to be in our grasp. Social media platforms like Facebook, Twitter, and Instagram are changing the way we see ourselves and the way we have relationships. We can create online communities or chat groups and instantly communicate with people across the world. With access to so many human connections you'd think loneliness

would be a thing of the past.

We've never been lonelier.

Katherine Hobson, citing a study released in 2017, reports,

> It turns out that the people who reported spending the most time on social media—more than two hours a day—had twice the odds of perceived social isolation than those who said they spent a half hour per day or less on those sites. And people who visited social media platforms most frequently, 58 visits per week or more, had more than three times the odds of perceived social isolation than those who visited fewer than nine times per week.

A friend said recently, "We can have a thousand friends on Facebook, but based on how we spend our time, it seems like Facebook is worth a thousand friends."

It's wrong though to place the blame for our social dislocation squarely on the shoulders of social media. Robert Putnam's famous book *Bowling Alone* describes the fragmentation and isolation of American community before the rise of social media. He says, "Americans are right that the bonds of our communities have withered and we are right to fear that this transformation has very real costs." Increasing loneliness, according to Putnam, has to do with the decrease in neighborhood societies, civic organizations, religious communities, and social clubs.

Loneliness is not just a modern problem. It's an ancient problem because it's a human problem. Ultimately, loneliness is a spiritual problem.

Not Good

A quick theological consideration of the problem of loneliness demonstrates its significance. In Genesis 2:18, God said, "It is not good that the man should be alone." The weight of this statement is even stronger when we remember the poetry of Genesis 1 that contains the refrain "God saw that it was good" seven times.

The repetition of the phrase alone is striking, but there are two additional amplifiers that we may not be aware of. First is the number of repetitions. In Hebrew the number seven is *sheba'*, a word identical in its consonantal root with *shaba'*, which means "to swear, as in to swear an oath." Seven is the sum of three (a biblical number suggesting glory, weightiness, or perfection) and four (a biblical number suggesting creation). In Isaiah 6, the cherubim sing "holy, holy, holy" to signify God's perfection in holiness, while the four corners of the earth and the four rivers flowing out of Eden signify the created order. The sum of three and four is thus meant to summon our attention. God saw and said that it was good seven times. The repetition and connotation emphasize and underline creation's goodness in the eyes of God. It's almost impossible to get a more emphatic statement, but we do.

Just in case we didn't catch the poem's refrain as it sang "it was good" seven times, we have a second amplifier, what in English is translated "very good." The English term *very* is a weak translation of the Hebrew term *me'od*. *Me'od* is defined first as "force, might" and second "to express the idea of exceedingly, greatly, very . . . Genesis 1:31 . . . good *exceedingly*." Creation is not just good. *It is exceedingly, abundantly, greatly, forcefully good.* This phrase gathers up all the earlier refrains from each "day" of creation that has come before. The Creator God beholds creation and describes it as exceedingly good.

Now consider again, "It is not good that the man should be alone" in Genesis 2:18. The contrast is like a verbal slap. The action breaks. It's the first point of tension in the whole narrative of Scripture. For humans to be alone is *not good*.

Anyone who has experienced loneliness knows this. Loneliness is a primal disorientation. Quiet anxiety gives way to restlessness. We look for distractions to numb ourselves and take the edge off. Anger and resentment simmer in successive waves.

Loneliness is no joke. Isolation is so powerfully disorienting that solitary confinement is classified as a form of torture.

As I sat in that chair across from Friar Ugo, I could feel the primordial weight of loneliness pressing in on me. I knew the story of Genesis 2. Not good that the man should be alone. So I thought, *God, fix it!* I wanted Friar Ugo to tell me how God was going to take the isolation away. Instead, he started talking about something else.

"Have you ever considered," he asked, "that the loneliness you're experiencing is an invitation to grow your friendship with God?"

I hadn't.

Friar Ugo went on, "Loneliness is part of the human condition. It is the experience of many around the corner who are living on the street. It is the experience of many around the world, separated from home, family, and land because of war or disease. And," he paused, "it was often the experience of our Lord himself. You can look to me . . . or to something else . . . even to religion to try to make you feel better. Or," he said, clearing his throat, "you could see this as the beginning of God's work of transformation in you."

And then we sat there in silence.

I pressed my lips together again, but something in his invitation had already stirred inside me. What if loneliness was a doorway to a deeper life with God? What would that mean? How might this idea reshape the experience?

After a short prayer our conversation ended. Friar Ugo didn't share stories of his isolation in ministry. He didn't talk, for example, about being forced to leave a country and a context he loved and not being allowed to return despite years of continued effort. He didn't describe his experience of returning to New York after forty years on the mission field. He simply prayed, and then I stepped out into the cold New York City morning with lots of questions. What would it look like to respond to God's invitation in the midst of loneliness? Was this a biblical idea? If so, what might Scripture have to teach about loneliness as a place of transformation?

To my surprise, the Old and New Testaments are full of examples of women and men who met God in the midst of loneliness or isolation.

- Abraham experienced loneliness in *his desire for family*: "Oh that Ishmael might live in your sight!" (Genesis 17:18).

- Moses experienced loneliness *when he fled Egypt*.

- Jacob experienced loneliness in the face of *his ambition*.

- Elijah faced loneliness in fatigue *after his great victory*.

- Nehemiah faced loneliness *in leadership* as he dealt with opposition from outside and sabotage within.

- Job experienced loneliness *in suffering* while his friends offered little comfort.

- Esther experienced loneliness *in the palace*: "But as for me, I have not been called to come in to the king these thirty days" (Esther 4:11 ESV).

- Mary chose loneliness in *her embrace of God's call*: "Behold, I am the servant of the Lord; let it be to me according to your word" (Luke 1:38 ESV).

- Paul experienced loneliness *in mission*.

- Ultimately Jesus experienced *the deepest loneliness of all* as he cried out, "My God, my God, why have you forsaken me?" (Matthew 27:46).

These stories reveal God's transforming presence and power in the lives of individuals and communities. They meet God in the midst of loneliness and are changed. Some walk away with a limp. Some walk away with deepened courage. The thought struck me, *What might I walk away with if I immersed myself in their stories?*

Turns out, we can learn a lot by sitting in the ashes with Job or in the wilderness with Hagar. God invites us into these stories, saying, "Wait with me." Entering these stories reframes our understanding of loneliness by demonstrating God's presence and purpose. It enlarges our heart to connect with the isolation of our spiritual forebears and perhaps to connect more deeply with others who face similar loneliness and isolation. Through these stories we are taught to hope in God's future.

Entering Scripture

To be transformed by these stories, however, meant being willing to enter them imaginatively and emotionally. This took a different approach to Scripture than I'd practiced before. Friar Ugo recommended a way of reading Scripture with the imagination and the intellect. Rather than simply observe, interpret, and apply insights (the inductive method of Scripture study that I continue to teach and use), imaginative reading goes further. It invites us to use observations about language, context, repetition, and conflict, and to place ourselves in the midst of the unfolding drama. We then imagine the story as a participant within rather than as an outside observer. Reading with the heart and imagination deepens learning and transforms the habits of heart and mind in ways that reading for information, understanding, and even moral exhortation does not.

For example, one of Jesus' most profound teachings is found in Luke 10:25-37, the parable of the good Samaritan. The parable emerges out of a lawyer's desire to experience the eternal life

Jesus was preaching about. He asks Jesus, "What must I do to inherit eternal life?" (v. 25). Jesus' response points out that the lawyer already knows the answer. If he wants to experience God's life, he needs to love God with everything he has and love his neighbor as himself.

Jesus' challenge, "Do this, and you will live" (v. 28) masterfully draws out the lawyer's real obstacle. Loving our neighbor as our self is much easier said than done. And so, as lawyers do, he asks Jesus to define his terms. "Who is my neighbor?" (v. 29).

What does this story look like from the inside if, for example, I imagine myself as the lawyer? Suddenly, I'm alert to the desire to have God's life. I imagine spending days wrestling with the Holy Book trying to accurately apply its insights to my life. I imagine a gnawing feeling in my gut that tells me I'm missing something. I long for God's life, not just for me but for my whole community. And I feel stuck. Then I imagine myself as the lawyer seeing Jesus. That he knows something about God's life is evident in the authority with which he speaks and heals. What is it? What does he know or understand about God's eternal life that I lack?

Placing myself inside the story helps me to see that the lawyer and I aren't that different. This means that the story of the good Samaritan is not simply a moral tale Jesus tells about being nice to those in need, but it's a key clarification of what it means to have life with God. It's as much Jesus' response to me in the twenty-first century as it was to this unnamed lawyer in the first.

The story of the good Samaritan does not answer the lawyer's question directly. Jesus describes a scenario where a wounded and vulnerable man is left on the side of the road to die. Religious experts notice the man and pass him by. In a remarkable twist, Jesus has the religious and ethnic outsider, a Samaritan, experience *splanchnizomai*, a graphic description of compassion, that literally means a movement or churning of the inner organs toward the wounded man. It's not just that the Samaritan "feels bad" for the wounded and vulnerable, he aches internally, seeing the earlier traveler's plight. This gut-wrenching compassion compels the Samaritan to act. The Samaritan, a man outside the law of God, disadvantages himself for the sake of this nameless, faceless other. Then comes the punchline, "Which of these three, do you think, was a neighbor to the man who fell into the hands of the robbers?" Jesus said (v. 36).

This story from Jesus answers the lawyer's question by reshaping the lawyer's and our definition of *neighbor*. *Neighbor* is not defined geographically, ethnically, or categorically, but by the compassion and activity of the one who sees others in need. According to Jesus, we do not first decide who our neighbor is and then practice hospitality, compassion, or mercy. We first practice hospitality, compassion, and mercy, and by so doing become a neighbor to those around us.

If I'm reading this story imaginatively, from the inside, I feel its sting. Do I experience *splanchnizomai* when I look out the window and see kids on the playground of the failing school across the street? Am I willing to disadvantage myself for them? What about the neighbor across the hall with a broken leg, the one fighting breast cancer, or the mom heartbroken about her son?

As I read from the inside, God's invitation becomes clear. Like the lawyer I want to justify myself. "Don't you see the people I'm hosting at my apartment every week? Don't you see the effort we're making to raise kids and build community? Why don't I feel like I'm experiencing eternal life?" Jesus' response, "Which one of these was a neighbor?" is as unsettling as it is beautiful. It touches the nerve of loneliness and invites ruthless self-examination. What if my "community building" activities are less about compassion for others and are instead motivated by a desire for acceptance, approval, or affection? What would it look like to "neighbor" others out of concern for their situation? As I ponder these questions, something like hope stirs inside. Even though today my love for my neighbor was self-serving, perhaps tomorrow, perhaps one day, I will be a neighbor and experience life with God in the ways I long for.

Invitation

It is not good for us to be alone. Yet in the hands of God loneliness can transform. If we learn to hear the invitation of God in loneliness, we can discover aspects of God's character, and ours, that are available no other way. If we meet God in loneliness, we can grow the desire and capacity to love others.

This book is an invitation to learn about God in the midst of loneliness by entering into Scripture. As you read, enter into these stories with your imagination. Let the tensions and puzzles of the characters create a space for you to articulate your own questions and tensions.

If you experience the ache of loneliness while you enter Scripture, slow down. Notice how it feels in your body. Notice what memories come up in your mind. Ask yourself, *How am I experiencing something like this in my life?* Read the chapter again and invite God to meet you in your memories, your experiences, and even the sensations you have in your body.

Remember not to judge your experience prematurely. Some of us have the tendency to associate all difficult emotion with sin. Anger, sadness, or fear, the emotions most basic to loneliness, are sometimes dismissed as unspiritual. They aren't. The Scriptures themselves are full of angry, sad, and scared prayers.

Consider David's prayer in Psalm 13,

How long, O LORD? Will you forget me forever?
How long will you hide your face from me?

How long must I bear pain in my soul,
    and have sorrow in my heart all day long?
How long shall my enemy be exalted over me? (vv. 1-2)

There is nothing unspiritual about complaining to God about situations and circumstances that feel unfair.

And consider this prayer breathed in the furnace of rage.

Rise up, O LORD!
    Deliver me, O my God!
For you strike all my enemies on the cheek;
    you break the teeth of the wicked. (Psalm 3:7)

If you are tempted to deny difficult emotions or distract yourself from them, I hope you'll experience these chapters as a safe place to name and pay attention to them instead. The biblical characters we'll reflect on in this book experience and express a host of difficult emotions in their life with God. When they voice these emotions, they do not sin but expose themselves more fully to God's transforming grace.

Each chapter will end with some questions for further reflection. Use these questions to go deeper into personal reflection or to guide and direct conversation with others.

It's been years since Friar Ugo and I sat together that cold morning. His words launched a spiritual quest. Could the experience of loneliness deepen my friendship with God? Could Scripture guide that process? Could the women and men on the pages of Scripture become mentors and allies along the way? Friar Ugo's invitation exposed parts of my heart that desperately needed to be confronted as well as comforted. His invitation enabled me to enter into Scripture in fresh and unexpected ways that warmed my heart, freed my imagination, illumined my mind, and expanded my desire for life with God.

What about you? Let's explore Scripture together and see if we can discover new depths of friendship with God. Your story is unique, but your experience of loneliness is profoundly human. To be human is to be lonely. But to discover friendship with God in the ache of loneliness is also deeply human. As one writer says, "Your desire for more of God than you have right now, your longing for love, your need for deeper levels of spiritual transformation than you have experienced so far is the truest thing about you."

Imagine how God might meet us as we explore the Scriptures together.

For Reflection and Discussion

As you experience seasons of loneliness, perhaps God has an invitation for you. The following are some questions to consider—now or later—on your own or with a group.

1. How has God used loneliness or isolation in my past to shape my character?

2. Which of the stories mentioned in this chapter resonate with my experiences?

3. What work might God be doing in me as I experience loneliness or isolation?

4. What do I wish God would do for me as I take time to reflect on his invitations?

2 | Leave

AN eleven-year-old faced with an adult decision looked out the airplane window and choked on the thought: *Will this be the last time I see palm trees?* Remembered beauty stung her eyes as she scanned the edges of the airfield for a palm tree to sear into memory. She felt and fought the urge to cry.

Mama slipped into her room earlier that morning. Her soft voice had steely undertones that made Sophia sit up straight. "I'm leaving for the States," she said directly. "You can stay here and possibly never see me again, or you can come with me and possibly never see this place again."

The airplane turned. Its engines raced. The palm trees were out of sight.

Many of us can relate to my wife's, Sophia's, story, even if our leaving home was less dramatic. A new job uproots a family. A marriage ends in divorce. A parent, sibling, dear friend, or spouse dies. Students go off to college. Home as we knew it is gone.

Need for work, political unrest, poverty, or violence also make people leave home. According to a UN document produced in 2012, worldwide there were 214 million displaced internationally and 740 million migrants who haven't yet left their home countries.

This is a staggering number of people. The UN document continues, "In total, therefore, about 1 billion persons, or one in seven, currently live outside their country or region of origin. These estimates are, however, conservative, as they do not include many persons migrating on a seasonal or temporary basis."

We long for home. Under the best of circumstances leaving home creates feelings of isolation, loneliness, and vulnerability. As a campus minister I've watched thousands of first-year students arrive on campus in September with bright eyes and wide smiles, yet by October they want to quit and return home. How much more distressing when we leave home under urgent and disorienting circumstances or when the relationship to our new home is tenuous. Jean Carlos Arce, a youth pastor in Los Angeles, describes his community: "The teenagers at our church are either first- or second-generation migrants from Latin America. Our migrant realities intersect at points—we miss our grandmother's cooking and the days where code-switching wasn't a thing—and diverge at others, namely, citizenship status."

Separation and Unity

The book of Genesis captures the hurt and the hope of leaving home. Three times in the book of Genesis God's calls his people to leave home. These invitations are beautiful, dreadful, and hopeful. Each call is accompanied by a poem that heightens the emotional resonance. When we reflect on God's command to leave home, we discover God's love and commitment toward the people he loves.

The first call to leave home comes in Genesis 2. The only tension in the story up to this point is in verse 18, "It is not good that the man should be alone; I will make him a helper as his partner." God then takes the man on a survey of the animal kingdom, allowing him to name each one. A quick reading of these verses seems a comical diversion, as though taking the ground creature, Adam, on safari would result in a cross-species partnership to resolve the challenge of loneliness. The point of this digression, however, is to reinforce the need for another human. "But for the man there was not found a helper as his partner" (v. 20).

Resolving the "not good" of the man being alone can only be done through a creature that has the "same flesh" as himself. Think typologically. The human creature may share common traits with animals but has a distinct type of flesh. The only way to overcome the aloneness inside this unique form of embodiment is another who shares in the same (or "one") flesh. And so God creates the woman out of the man's flesh and gives the man and woman to one another. They are to be one-flesh partners, image bearers, and keepers of creation.

Then comes the first invitation to leave home. Seeing the woman for the first time, the man breaks out into poetry.

This is now bone of my bones
    and flesh of my flesh;
she shall be called "woman,"
    for she was taken out of man.

That is why a man leaves his father and mother and is united
to his wife, and they become one flesh. (vv. 23-24 NIV)

This invitation to separation and unity is where the narrative has been driving all along. By separating woman from man, sexing (used as a verb) humankind, God resolves the tension of the story. The man is not alone. There is no longer one but two living souls. Separation allows relationship. Without an "other" who shares the capacity for language, knowledge, reason, and relationship with God, the man would be forever alone. This human other is distinct in body, consciousness, perspective, and will. Difference creates the opportunity for discovery. Woman and man are like but not like. They are the same but different. The man is no longer alone. It is no longer "not good."

This primal relationship bends back toward unity. Woman is separated from man in order to be reunited with him. Male and female are made to be one-flesh helpers to one another. The physical, relational, and spiritual union enables woman and man to produce children "in their image," who will reflect the image of God further into creation. In this way the act of sexing, separating, uniting, and creating enables woman and man to accomplish their created purpose: reflecting the creative, generative love of God.

This picture is inescapably poetic. It's the rhythm of same and different in a unified whole that hearkens back to the poetry of Genesis 1, where night and day, light and dark, earth and sea, sun and moon all present themselves as distinct, interdependent parts of creation bringing delight to the Creator.

This invitation to leave home is meant to heal loneliness. In this ideal marital union, the man and woman are most profoundly not alone. This relationship is about knowing and being known. It's about creating life, patterns, and culture. Loneliness and isolation are no more. The couple is naked and unashamed. Leaving home in this sense was meant to be beautiful.

While no marriage or relationship lives up to the vision of Genesis 2, echoes of longing for its beauty abound. A popular song from the movie *The Greatest Showman* captures this echo.

There's a house we can build
Every room inside is filled . . .
The special things I compile
Each one there to make you smile.

This song occupies a primary place in the musical. It comes just after the overture and introduces us to the main characters and their desires. The rest of the musical centers on whether or not this couple is able to realize their dreams and build this beautiful home together. *The Greatest Showman* is a story with many themes: showmanship, wonder, class consciousness, racialization, marginalization, and beauty, to name a few, but none of these are what the musical is about. It's about a man and a woman and their dream of building a beautiful home together. It's what keeps us watching.

In the song, Charity and Phineas press against familiar boundaries of home and routine. We share their delight as they help each other realize the dream. We trace their dancing with our eyes and see two become one in purpose and in posture. This is Genesis 2 longing.

It's not just romantic love. Genesis 2 is clear that a suitable helper is needed. The Hebrew term is *'ezer* and is much more robust than English translations connote. In the Old Testament the word *'ezer* most often refers to God. It is derived from root sounds meaning both power and strength. The woman is created to have power and strength corresponding to and of the same flesh as man. This is an image not of subservience but of authority and ability.

Therefore, the beautiful longing in God's invitation to leave home doesn't just apply to married couples. In the best friendships, we recognize the friend as an "other" whose *power and strength* increases our capacity to learn, love, or leave a mark on creation. We see the longing realized in the story of a single woman or man who discovers a community through which their work, creativity, and authority combine to create something meaningful. A vision of *'ezer* is experienced in active retirees who invest in other people's children. It can apply to a scholar, artisan, teacher, entrepreneur, missionary, or a monastic.

Where do you experience this beautiful longing to leave home and lend your power and strength to create something good?

What stirs in you as you contemplate discovering relationships in which you can know and be known? How do you understand your call to marriage or singleness in this season?

You Can't Go Home Again

While beautiful, this poetic call to leave home describes our longings far more than our actual experience. Leaving home hurts. The call to leave conjures at least as much dread as delight. God's second command to leave home in Genesis describes this dynamic well.

> Then the LORD God said, "See, the man has become like one of us, knowing good and evil; and now, he might reach out his hand and take also from the tree of life, and eat, and live forever"—therefore the LORD God sent him forth from the garden of Eden, to till the ground from which he was taken. He drove out the man; and at the east of the garden of Eden he placed the cherubim, and a sword flaming and turning to guard the way to the tree of life. (Genesis 3:22-24)

The beautiful invitation to leave father and mother to be united in marriage gives way to horror as the man and woman turn from God, turn on each other, and infect the ground with their disobedience. They are turned out of the garden. They can no longer approach the tree of life. Woman and man can't go back home.

Life east of Eden isolates. Relationships that were bending toward unity are now pushing against one another. Woman and man are clothed with skins to hide their shame. The man and woman hide from one another. They are no longer able to endure seeing and being seen, knowing and being known. The man, whose first response to seeing the woman is to describe her as "bone of my bones and flesh of my flesh," now names the woman, perhaps as he has named the animals, calling her Eve or "mother."

This is a significant turn and shift away from the man's first poem. Being a mother is merely one of the woman's many potential strong and powerful contributions. Why is it that women still struggle to have their strength, contribution, and same flesh recognized by men?

We see the isolating consequences of sin in the second poem. Eve's poem in response to the birth of her son Cain says, "I have produced a man with the help of the LORD" (Genesis 4:1). There's a play on words in this simple verse of poetry. The name Cain connotes power and authority and is related to the verb "to acquire" or "to create." In English we might say, "I have made a maker" or "I have produced a producer."

The emphasis of Genesis 4:1 celebrates Eve's accomplishment as an individual. There is no "bone of my bones, flesh of my flesh" unity captured here. Mother is producer. Son is produced. The man "knew his wife" but is otherwise strangely absent. East of Eden, relationships are filled with ambiguity. There's shame. East of Eden, loneliness reemerges as unity dissolves into disconnection, distrust, and ultimately death.

If life east of Eden is so isolating, why would God command it? Why force the couple to leave home? Is this some kind of punishment or curse?

Sometimes it's better to leave home.

While violence wasn't a constant in my home, the threat of it lingered like stale cigarette smoke. Terror slinked up my spine when I'd turn around to see one of my stepbrothers swinging a hatchet toward the back of my head. My chest started to pound when I'd hear my dad and sister arguing over housework. One time I'd been foolish enough to insert myself between the two of them and punched my dad several times in the ribs. The next thing I knew I was hunched over on the couch gasping for breath.

Something broke inside me late one afternoon. A family member had asked me to help him fix part of his motorcycle engine. I agreed but went to a friend's house instead. When I came home the house was full of silent fury. Words turned into punches. To my shock as much as his, I avoided his first punch. Instead of taking the punch as I'd expected to, I managed to move to his right side, wrap his right arm, and hip-toss him, creating space between us. "This isn't over!" he shouted and ran downstairs.

The room went dark. My mind fixated on the imaginary prospect of a figure returning with a hatchet, hammer, or another of the woodworking tools we kept in the basement. The only light I could see was the path to the back door. The only thought I could think was the simple command, run.

I bolted out the door, through backyards, and through a patch of woods, anything to put more space between me and the violence I'd just experienced and the escalation I was afraid would come. I couldn't go home.

Was my leaving home a punishment or curse? By no means! There are times when home is so unstable, frightening, and dangerous that the best thing to do is leave. The command to leave the first couple's garden home can be seen as God's blessing and provision. Hands that grasp after independence, autonomy, and power can't be trusted to bear the weight of interdependence. The tree of life, which before represented abundance and health, now represents a temptation. Imagine humans forever trapped in a grasping, shaming, blaming, and fearful relationship toward God and one another.

When home is no longer safe, leaving may be best for us. God's second command to leave home reveals his desire to protect his people, to cover their shame even in the dissonance of life east of

Eden. Ignatius of Loyola recognized this as a pivotal component of developing friendship with God.

Commenting on the *Spiritual Exercises* of St. Ignatius, Patti Clement writes,

> If we feel a disorder in our attachment to a person, to a job
> or position, to a certain dwelling place, a certain city, country,
> and so on, we should take it to the Lord and pray insistently
> to be given the grace to free ourselves from such disorder.
> What we want above all is the ability to respond freely to
> God, and all other loves for people, places, and things are
> held in proper perspective by the light and strength of
> God's grace.

Abraham: Blessing

God's third command to leave home in Genesis restores hope. The Lord said to Abram, "Go from your country and your kindred and your father's house to the land that I will show you" (Genesis 12:1).

This is no small command. In a highly mobile and individualized culture we're prone to miss how significant God's call to leave home was for Abram. Where we're from matters. The topology, climate, and history of a place have lasting significance for the people who live there. Often this significance is so thoroughly integrated into the mindset of those who live there that to state it explicitly is like announcing that water is wet.

For example, New York City's naturally deep harbors made it an ideal location for European traders to set up shop during the age of colonialization. New York was unique among New World cities of its age, being founded by Europeans (first the Dutch, then the English) entirely for the purpose of trade and economic opportunity. Almost four hundred years later New York City, especially Manhattan, is still economically anchored around trading global commodities, now done efficiently through the stock market. New Yorkers know that time is money. Sinatra and Alicia Keys laud New York as the place of making dreams and opportunities. These sentiments are not cultural oddities, they are the cumulative impact of land and history.

Embedded in the call to leave home, then, is an invitation to reconsider the internalized assumptions of place and history. Friends who have left New York City confess, "The pace and intense competitiveness of the city are addictive. It took me a few years to settle into different rhythms. I'm glad I did."

What did Abram's leaving Ur and Haran give him the ability to reconsider or discover? We can only speculate. Ur and Haran were centers for worship of the moon god Nanna/Sin. Abram's leaving home certainly caused him to reexamine his understanding of God.

For Abram the call to leave home also meant he would be an exile, cut off from familiar people, language, customs, and even family. In traditional cultures, family is everything. If you ask my mother-in-law who she is, she will not tell you about her presidential award, ongoing charity work, faith, or children. Instead, she will tell you about her parents, their parents, and the overlapping family network spanning back generations. This is how she describes others in the family as well.

As someone who grew up in the United States, I find this dizzying. "You remember your Tita Connie?" *No*, I think. "She's the daughter of Roberto and Maria, on the Robledo side." I still haven't a clue. She keeps going. She will name every direct and indirect family connection going back three generations. This isn't a quirk. From her perspective, family, geography, and history tell you who you are. In individualistic West, we may struggle to understand this, but family name, history, and honor are important where memories are long and life uncertain.

In Genesis 11 we're introduced to nine generations of Abram's family. This is ancient storytelling 101. The reader or hearer of this genealogy knows that at the end of this list of names we're going to be introduced to someone who is going to move the action or story forward in a particular way. The reader or listener knows that this character's actions will bring either honor or shame to the whole family. Nobody expects that next line to be "Go . . . from your kindred and your father's house."

God continues his call to leave home with a promise.

> I will make you into a great nation,
>> and I will bless you;
> I will make your name great,
>> and you will be a blessing.
> I will bless those who bless you,
>> and whoever curses you I will curse;
> and all peoples on earth
>> will be blessed through you. (Genesis 12:2-3 NIV)

This time it's the Lord communicating in poetry. The repetition of "I will" identifies God as the main actor. If we make a sentence out of the words that are repeated five times in this poem, we get the simple kernel sentence "I will bless you." Taken together the message of God to Abram is, "Leave home. I will bless you."

Leaving home is hard. It's lonely. We long for the comfort of what's familiar. We fear isolation and dissonance. Too many of us have been driven out of home by violence, desperation, or need. What blessing could possibly await those who leave home?

Leaving home marks the beginning of Abram's life with God. From the time the woman and man are expelled from the garden in Genesis, the human inclination is to rebel against God and be violent toward one another. Cain, celebrated in Eve's poem at his birth, becomes the first murderer. Human cruelty and violence multiply. God brings judgment. Human pride and vanity multiply. God brings judgment. The trajectory of the relationship between human beings and God seems to be set on a hopeless course. Then God calls Abram. Everything changes. By leaving home, Abram begins a long journey of friendship with God.

As I read the story of Abram imaginatively, the opportunity and weight of Abram's call comes crashing in on me. What might it mean to leave home in order to cultivate friendship with God? Is it possible that God is offering a poem of blessing through Abram that speaks to my sense of dislocation?

The rest of the Bible is the story of God's promise to Abram worked out in time and history. His story is our story. It is a story with many challenges. There are promising vistas and dark seasons. In the fullness of time Jesus, too, would leave home in order to take up our humanity. He would leave home in Galilee for an itinerant ministry. He would leave home for an excruciating death on a cross so God's blessing could go to the whole world.

Thirteen years after her eyes scanned the airfield for palm trees, Sophia and I touched down at Ninoy Aquino International Airport in Manila. We'd been married just under one month. Her shoulders tensed as she looked out the window. The palm trees were still there. She let out the breath she hadn't realized she was holding. She shared her story like a confession.

In the years since we were in Manila, I've reflected on that moment. In it, I hear the echoes of Genesis and the call of God. Not a day goes by that I don't look at Sophia and think of Adam's "bone of my bones and flesh of my flesh" poetry. This is less romantic than it sounds. Building a life together requires our best efforts. It's business meetings, chores, and dishes as much as poetry and long walks, but there's an echo of joy and richness that is ancient and primordial. In this relationship Sophia and I touch God's gift with slippery fingers, but it's there.

Not a day goes by when we're not aware that we can't go home again. The shadow of tough decisions made too young hangs overhead. We all live downstream of the decisions made by sinful people all the way back to the first woman and man. We contribute to those sinful decisions in ways we aren't even aware of. We laugh. We cry. We hurt each other. We lean on God's generosity and provision.

Not a day goes by in which we're not called to blessing. We create rhythms of life in which we can know God and inspire others to know God. This requires us to reevaluate the stories and expectations we grow up with. It means leaving traditions, people, and places behind. And it means entering friendship with God.

For Reflection and Discussion

1. How might God be inviting you to leave home?

2. As you consider the three different calls to leave home in Genesis, which stood out most to you? How do you relate? What emotional responses does it awaken in you?

3. Are there destructive relationships and places God is calling you to leave? If so, what are they?

4. What hope or blessing do you long for as you leave home? How might you turn that into a prayer?

3 | Desert

I think there's a giving-up tax," Rich said as we loaded boxes and furniture into a rented truck. Each box was weighed down by deferred hopes and the crushing sense of failure.

I've helped a lot of friends move. I even spent one summer moving furniture as a full-time job. Rich's move was the most surreal. We'd be carrying a couch or desk, something that needs to be carefully negotiated around corners and stairwells, and Rich would go limp. It was as though the simple act of needing to think about how to position a piece of furniture was too much for him. He couldn't think. He couldn't talk. He couldn't process simple instructions. Then, we'd finally get the piece loaded into the truck, and Rich would stare at it as though he didn't quite know how that desk or armchair had gotten there.

Rich had moved to Harlem inspired to change the world. He'd started an organization. He'd raised funds. He worked with local people, incorporated feedback, and began to do truly innovative and inspiring work. Two years later, betrayed and broke, Richard was closing up shop.

His sense of failure surrounded him like a bubble. He felt alone.

Rising Anxiety

Entrepreneurial author Seth Godin shrewdly describes anxiety as "repeatedly re-experiencing failure in advance." This paralyzing sense of anxiety is on the rise among young people. More than half of the students using counseling services at US colleges and universities are dealing with anxiety. Benoit Denizet-Lewis wrote in the *New York Times,*

> Over the last decade, anxiety has overtaken depression as the most common reason college students seek counseling services. In its annual survey of students, the American College Health Association found a significant increase—to 62 percent in 2016 from 50 percent in 2011—of under-graduates reporting "overwhelming anxiety" in the previous year. Surveys that look at symptoms related to anxiety are also telling. In 1985, the Higher Education Re-search Institute at U.C.L.A. began asking incoming college freshmen if they "felt overwhelmed by all I had to do" during the previous year. In 1985, 18 percent said they did. By 2010, that number had increased to 29 percent. Last year, it surged to 41 percent.

The pressure to perform, to succeed, to "make it" turns potential friends into rivals and learning opportunities into crushing defeats. This isolates us and makes us lonely. How do we connect with others while overwhelmed by dreams breaking in front of us like a stack of broken dishes in the sink? How do we build friendships while feeling like a fraud? How do we reach out while overwhelmed?

God's response to human anxiety, vulnerability, and fear of failure is to meet us in the desert. The desert is a place of profound vulnerability. It is a place fraught with dangers physical, emotional, and spiritual. The invitation to the desert is not comfortable. It's counterintuitive.

The desert purges. The desert exposes. The desert reveals.

Belden Lane writes, "The God of Sinai is one who thrives on fierce landscapes, seemingly forcing God's people into wild and wretched climes where trust must be absolute."

God meets Hagar twice in the desert in the midst of her anxiety, oppression, and despondency. Hagar's story resonates with those who've felt the sting of injustice. It is a painful story of a woman blessed by God in the midst of shouldering the weight of others' bad decisions. Moses flees Egypt a failure and fugitive. His story resonates with those whose dreams have turned to dust. In both of these stories we see God's intervention in the desert. It's a challenging path. No one who walks through the desert and meets God returns the same.

Entering the Tension

In college I took and almost failed a directing class. It was a graduate-level course with the professor, Dr. Martin (like the shoes), Tom, Claudia, and me. Our final project was a director's notebook that included set design work, scene study, production-cost estimates, costume sketches, lighting schematics, and anticipated acting challenges. The discipline of the assignment was to link all of our directing choices to a thesis, a vision of the play we were hoping to draw out physically.

Inspired by the musical adaptation of *Don Quixote*, I began to work. I dumped hours into the project. It was the most work I'd done for a single class. My particular vision was steeped in idealism. "The ideal is better than the real" was like a slogan on page after page of the notebook. At the midpoint of the semester I submitted a draft. Dr. Martin's comments stung. "I appreciate your idealism. But, you have not engaged with any of the complexities and moral ambiguities of the play. It's the tensions, mixed and competing objectives, and unresolved conflicts that theatre explores. You do not need to eliminate your perspective, but you must start over and engage what real tensions exist in the play or you will fail the class."

Entering Hagar's story is like entering a piece of good theater. *Good* characters make *bad* decisions; no one is a full-time hero. God is at work in the tensions, competing objectives, and unresolved conflicts.

The story of Hagar is painfully dissonant. Understandably so. In this brief story we see the further subjugation of women. Women have descended from creation in power and strength corresponding to men to a world where two women, Sarah and Hagar, are treated as property.

The dissonance in this text was not just a tension point for modern readers. Ancient commentators wrestled with Abraham and Sarah's apparent sin. This suggests that we shouldn't come to this text expecting the characters to behave with perfect justice, compassion, and virtue. The narrative about Sarah and Hagar is layered with moral ambiguities, human failure, injustice, anxiety, and despondency. This is an advantage. It moves the story out of the category of morality tale and anchors it in the complexities of real human life.

Hagar: Meeting God in the Desert

Hagar's story begins just after the call of Abraham, which we discussed in chapter two, when Abraham and Sarah traveled to Egypt (Genesis 12). Sarah was physically beautiful. Abraham feared powerful Egyptian men would kill him in order to take Sarah, so Abraham lies about being married to her. As a result, Sarah is taken into Pharaoh's house. Unnamed, this is likely also where Abraham acquired Hagar. When Sarah joined Pharaoh's household, Pharaoh gave Abraham, "sheep, oxen, male donkeys, male and female slaves, female donkeys, and camels" (v. 16).

Imagine the vulnerability Sarah endured. Imagine being given to another man by your husband. *The Women's Bible Commentary* captures a sense of the injustice in the narrative.

> This text does not tell of Sarah's reaction to the plan. Only Abraham's emotional state and speech are recorded. Sarah's status in this transaction is as his property. She has no say in the arrangements, and we learn nothing of Sarah's response to becoming the wife of a man she does not know. He (Abraham) is the subject of the story; she is an object.

The Scriptures do not bring us into Sarah's experience. Its silence is difficult to interpret. But God does not leave Sarah in her vulnerability. "The story would end here, and we would hear no more of Sarah, if it were not for God's intervention. Abraham treats Sarah as disposable, but God does not." God acts on Sarah's behalf, bringing diseases on Pharaoh's household and allowing the truth to come to light.

What do we make of Abraham, a man chosen to share in a covenant of God, treating his wife with such disregard? How do we, in a culture where women's bodies are still objectified for commercial benefit, understand these sets of decisions? Should we read the text as misogynistic because of the absence of Sarah's perspective or as liberating to women given God's action on Sarah's behalf?

The story makes clear that Abraham, the father of faith, is fearful and faithless when it comes to Sarah. This is a failure on the part of Abraham. God has promised to bless him and make him a blessing. But Abraham's anxiety, deception, and faithlessness to Sarah do not align with God's promise. Sarah unfairly bears the weight of Abraham's fear. His anxiety has real consequences for her. She is betrayed and exposed. The Egyptians send Abraham and Sarah away in order to rid themselves of the disease

Abraham's deception brought about. This is hardly Abraham being a "blessing to the nations."

I can't imagine what it'd be like for Sarah. The closest experience I ever had to this kind of rejection happened at my stepbrother's wedding. I was seated at a table with my brother and sister when my dad stood up to make a toast. "I just want you to know," Dad said to my stepbrother and to the gathered guests, "that you are my real son. You are far more to me than any of my natural kids." The air around me got heavy. I sat motionless. What was I hearing? Did my dad really just publicly announce that the same kid I fled from in terror was his real son? Where did that leave me?

Imagine Sarah, like my friend Rich, packing up to leave Egypt. Imagine her cocooned by a sense of betrayal and isolation. Imagine Sarah trying to make sense of God's call to Abraham and his family, while anxiously wondering where she really fit. Imagine the anxiety to produce an heir—to secure her place in the family—as urgent and fearful. Ten years go by and still no son. God promises that Abraham will have a son of his own to be his heir (see Genesis 15). What will this mean for childless, once-betrayed Sarah?

> Now Sarai, Abram's wife, bore him no children. She had an Egyptian slave-girl whose name was Hagar, and Sarai said to Abram, "You see that the LORD has prevented me from bearing children; go in to my slave-girl; it may be that I shall obtain children by her." And Abram listened to the voice of Sarai. So, after Abram had lived ten years in the land of Canaan, Sarai, Abram's wife, took Hagar the Egyptian, her slave-girl, and gave her to her husband Abram as a wife. He went in to Hagar, and she conceived; and when she saw that she had conceived, she looked with contempt on her mistress. Then Sarai said to Abram, "May the wrong done to me

be on you! I gave my slave-girl to your embrace, and when she saw that she had conceived, she looked on me with contempt. May the LORD judge between you and me!" But Abram said to Sarai, "Your slave-girl is in your power; do to her as you please." Then Sarai dealt harshly with her, and she ran away from her. (Genesis 16:1-6)

Ten years after Sarah was *given* to Pharaoh, she repeats the pattern. Sarah *gives* her slave girl, Hagar, to her husband in the hope that she would conceive a child. The ambiguities and tensions within the story become more pronounced. On one hand it was common practice at the time. "Documents from ancient Mesopotamia contain marriage agreements that state that if a wife was not able to bear children, then she was responsible for providing her husband with a surrogate." On the other hand, it's easy to read Sarah's actions as a passing on of the trauma she received in Egypt. In Egypt she had been an object to be traded for Abraham's personal safety and economic advantage. Now, she's objectifying Hagar to satisfy her own need to produce a child for her husband and so secure her position in the household. Hagar has no choice in this arrangement. She is a tool, an object.

Hagar's conceiving a child increases the complexity and tensions of the story. Hagar, perhaps understandably, feels contempt toward Sarah for giving her to Sarah's husband. Perhaps she experiences some pride at being able to succeed where her mistress has failed. Sarah, meanwhile, experiences vulnerability because of the possibility of being replaced by this younger woman. It's a mess! Sarah mistreats Hagar, and Hagar flees into the desert.

Hagar's anxious flight into the desert was the result of injustice. Her story is echoed in the experience of one out of every two hundred people in the world today who live in slavery. Here is "Patricia's" story as told by Restore NYC, an organization working with sex-trafficking victims.

> Patricia was sold to a local gang at the age of 16 because her parents could not afford to support their family. She was trafficked at a cantina in her rural community in Central America before being brought to New York by an abusive boyfriend. Once here, he moved Patricia from one brothel to another. She had no contact with her family and never had enough time in any one brothel to form friendships. Other than her relationship with her trafficker, she was completely alone.
>
> Patricia was trafficked in this way for almost a decade. While being trafficked, she gave birth to Marta and Luis. When Luis was one, Patricia reached out to an organization serving domestic-violence victims. She was identified as a trafficking victim.

The injustice of Patricia's story as with Hagar's story stirs something deep within us, even if we've never experienced such injustice ourselves. We can imagine, with horror, being cut off from family and friends. We can imagine being afraid and uncertain about our future. We can imagine longing to escape unhealthy and abusive relationships while simultaneously fearing the unknown.

Hagar flees to the desert. Here, alone in the desert, Hagar has her first encounter with God.

God's words to Hagar echo his promise to Abraham. There is a powerful play on words throughout this interaction. The name Ishmael means, "God hears." By instructing Hagar to name her son Ishmael, God is saying, "I *hear* your cry in the midst of injustice." God promises to bless her son and make their family into a great nation despite the opposition, oppression, and challenge that will mark Ishmael's life. In response Hagar names God El-roi, literally "God sees me." God's words and interactions with Hagar have given her agency and dignity.

God notices Hagar. He sees her in her flight, fear, and anxiety. God cares for her, affirms that he's listening, and promises to bless her. While we might be surprised that God's message to Hagar sends her back to Sarah, it's possible to see God's provision for Hagar even in this act. On her own Hagar would be even more vulnerable. By sending her back to Abraham and Sarah, Hagar and her son would be provided for.

God's promise to provide for Hagar and her son is tested in Hagar's second flight into the desert. After Sarah gives birth to Isaac, she asks Abraham to send Hagar and Ishmael away so they will not threaten Isaac's inheritance. Even though Abraham is distressed by this request, he nevertheless sends Hagar and Ishmael away. This time the water runs out. They are exposed and alone. Hagar leaves her son under a bush because she is afraid to watch him die of dehydration (Genesis 21:15-16).

There are layers to Hagar's grief. As a mother she is rightly heartbroken as she witnesses her son weakening in the heat of the desert, but Ishmael isn't the only one at death's door. Where is the God who sees? What about the promise to make her the mother of a multitude? Was it all a mirage?

Rich was asking questions like Hagar's as he packed up that truck. Was he a fool to have followed what he understood to be God's call to Harlem? Did God abandon him? Would Rich ever be able to risk again? What was Rich going to do now that his project had failed?

In the midst of fears and unanswered questions God meets Hagar in the desert.

As she sat opposite him, she lifted up her voice and wept. And God heard the voice of the boy; and the angel of God called to Hagar from heaven, and said to her, "What troubles you, Hagar? Do not be afraid; for God has heard the voice of the boy where he is. Come, lift up the boy and hold him fast with your hand, for I will make a great nation of him." Then God opened her eyes and she saw a well of water. She went, and filled the skin with water, and gave the boy a drink. (Genesis 21:16-19)

This time God's word confirms the promise and provides what is needed to sustain them. Hagar's story ends here, but God's promise holds true. Ishmael grows and becomes the father of a great nation. Hagar has met God twice in the desert. Her story illuminates and contrasts the story of Abraham in powerful ways. Where Abraham and Sarah sought their own stability resulting in injustice, Hagar embraces her vulnerability. Hagar meets God not in her accomplishments or schemes but in the arid desert landscape of nothing left to lose. Sarah is anxious to protect an inheritance for Isaac. Hagar receives an inheritance she didn't look for or try to control. Hagar attends to the voice of God with simple faith. She does not laugh or question God's promise. She does not abuse others to get what she wants. She is transformed by the presence of God met in the desert.

Desert Spirituality

The gift of meeting God in the desert is humility. Hagar, through the desert, moves from the anxiety caused by injustice and oppression to simple obedience to the voice of the God who sees and hears her, the God who meets her in the desert. In the third century, desert spirituality came into fresh expression. St. Anthony of Egypt and the many who followed him saw the fearful desert as a place where anxiety could be burned away. In its place, followers of Jesus could cultivate the gift of humility.

The humility of the desert is not self-indulgent, self-loathing scrupulosity. The desert unmasks this as a manifestation of pride. It tears away our self-exaltation and our self-pity. Humility, in this desert tradition, is the growing capacity to love as God loves. On the other side of loss, emptiness, and vulnerability is a love greater than death. The desert invites us to know this love even as it strips us bare.

In his book *The Solace of Fierce Landscapes*, Belden Lane captures this truth about learning to love through the purging away of other attachments.

> The sixteenth-century Spanish Carmelite reformer John of the Cross came to understand this truth during nine months of solitary confinement in a dark Toledo prison cell. We find ourselves truly free and capable of loving God, he argued, only as we experience the deprivation of all other things we may have depended upon for comfort, security, and self-esteem. What happens when one is suddenly stripped of everything that lends meaning to life—reputation, the worth of one's work, father, mother, the familiarity of one's home?

Hagar is the first biblical character I think of when I reflect on desert spirituality. She was treated unfairly by the father and mother of the faith. The injustice of it is infuriating. Hearing God's voice in the desert does not take injustice away or justify it.

Hagar is a hero though because of the way her character is transformed by the God who sees her. When we first meet Hagar, she views Sarah with justifiable contempt. When we last see her, she is primarily concerned for her son. She does not scheme, fight, or flail. She does not grasp. She is faithful and free. Hagar lives in response to God's love and faithfulness despite oppression and vulnerability; she is stripped of everything except the God who sees her.

I got my first professional acting job when I was a teenager. Growing up in western Massachusetts, the opportunities for acting weren't overwhelming, but I got by. By the time I was in college, I was making a living by cobbling together acting work and other platform skill work (emceeing, storytelling, interpretation, singing, and so forth). Then in 1996, all but one job dried up. I was desperate to find new opportunities, so I auditioned across the country. I auditioned at repertory theaters and off-Broadway, for touring companies, even for graduate and actor training programs. Nothing happened.

It was totally disorienting. I'd never struggled to book a job like that before. I'd always been able to book something. The months went on. I felt humiliated. I remember the taste of carpet where I sobbed uncontrollably after my final rejection notice came. It was my first taste of desert spirituality.

Moses: Journey to Humility

We don't often think of it this way, but Moses' leadership story begins in failure. In Moses' youth he goes out to see his people, the Hebrews, and discovers their forced labor. Moses acts to liberate them by killing one of the taskmasters. The next day Moses is rejected by two of his fellow Hebrews as he attempts to intervene in a dispute and discovers they know he had murdered an Egyptian. Moses flees Egypt in fear for his life (Exodus 2:11-15). Moses did not lighten the burden of his people or earn their respect. Not only does he fail to free his people, but he also becomes a fugitive in the wilderness.

God's call to Moses in Exodus 3 happens after years in the desert. Moses' experience as a failed liberator has hardened like scales over his heart. Once upon a time Moses was ready to kill Egyptian taskmasters and lead the Hebrews. Now he pleads with God to send someone else. Moses' ambition to be the liberating hero has been stripped away by years of shepherding in the wilderness. As one who had been raised by Pharaoh's daughter, Moses would have seen shepherding as an abhorrent profession, something beneath his talent and education (Genesis 46:34). Year after year Moses wanders in the wilderness caring for sheep, his pride burning away in the arid land. Moses is doing dirty work for someone else. There is little trace of the self-important Hebrew liberator left.

The tension in the conversation between God and Moses in the burning bush is about humility. Many years after Moses' failure, God comes with a promise of liberation exceeding the younger Moses' hopes and dreams. Moses asks, "Who am I that I should go to Pharaoh, and bring the Israelites out of Egypt?" (Exodus 3:11). Then begins a series of negotiations in which Moses attempts to secure information, resources, signs, God's name: anything he can use to avoid the vulnerability of going back to Egypt, that place of failure and emptiness. Moses has let go of his pride, but he does not yet know God. He does not recognize God as "the God who sees," despite the fact that God's self-disclosure includes these pointed words, "I have observed the misery of my people who are in Egypt; I have heard their cry on account of their taskmasters. Indeed, I know their sufferings" (Exodus 3:7). In order to gain humility, Moses needs to know God and recognize him as the one who sees.

God promises Moses that "I will be with you." This movement from fear and failure to humility, the ability to love as God loves, is the inward journey of Moses for the rest of his life. In Moses' outer journey he accomplishes great things. Moses leads the people out of Egypt, demonstrates God's holiness, delivers the law, and builds the tabernacle, the center of Israelite worship. Moses' inner journey is marked by an increasing attentiveness to life and friendship with God. Moses speaks to God "as one speaks to a friend" (Exodus 33:11).

Moses' story becomes the main text for desert spirituality. Fourth-century bishop Gregory of Nyssa's book *The Life of Moses* is a classic of Christian spirituality. Gregory sees in Moses' story a movement up the mountain toward deeper contemplation of God. He summons us to life with God, ever seeking to know God, ever only glimpsing God's back, ever called to move closer.

A story from the desert tradition captures this well.

> When Abba Macarius [a monk in the desert tradition] was returning from the marsh to his cell [the place where monks lived] one day carrying some palm leaves, he met the devil on the road with a scythe. The latter struck at him as much as he pleased, but in vain, and he said to him, "What is your power, Macarius, that makes me so powerless against you? All that you do, I do too; you fast, so do I; you keep vigil, and I do not sleep at all; in one thing only do you beat me." Abba Macarius asked what that was. He said, "Your humility. Because of that, I can do nothing against you."

The desert calls us to humility, the ability to love as God loves. Being with God in the desert frees us from the crushing weight of failure and the anxieties that paralyze. True humility, the gift of the desert, frees us from the need for approval, validation, security, and success. The journey into the desert is painful. Janis Joplin once sang, "Freedom's just another word for nothing left to lose." The line is insightful. We cling to a vision of success, honor, and security without realizing these visions anchor our hearts in vainglory, pride, and resentment. Meeting God in the desert strips these visions bare. It gives us humility, the ability to love as God loves: fearless, generous, and free.

For Reflection and Discussion

1. How would you describe your current level of worry, anxiety, or fear? What vision or value feels vulnerable?

2. How have experiences of injustice, betrayal, or rejection shaped your ability to connect with and trust others?

3. Have you ever had something that you'd consider a desert experience? What attachments or fears felt threatened? In what ways might God have been at work?

4. This chapter defines humility as "to love as God loves." What about that invitation inspires or troubles you? How might you grow in love this week?

4 | Grasp

THE American dream inspires millions to grasp after opportunities for social advancement, wealth, status, influence, and fame. But grasping after wealth, fame, or authority is risky. Loneliness is the dark underbelly of ambition.

Entrepreneur Jason Duff wrote,

I felt the worst at the exact moment I was being recognized the most.

On the outside, I was celebrated as a successful entrepreneur. I had built several multimillion-dollar businesses that employed hundreds of people in my local community.

On the inside, everything was falling apart. Under extreme stress, I was sleeping four hours per night and neglecting my most important relationships. As a result, I developed debilitating acid reflux. Not only did I have surgery and go on daily medication, it was so painful to speak that I could only whisper.

I was 25.

I can't read Jason Duff's words without thinking about another Jason. Jason Raize was the singularly most-talented singer I ever had the privilege to call my friend. By twenty-two Jason had won a Tony Award, been on the cover of national magazines and on daytime TV, and engaged in global charity work. By twenty-eight Jason would be desperately alone.

Is grasping ambition the path to our dreams or the path to loneliness? What invitation does God have for Jason Duff or Jason Raize? What invitation does God have for me in the midst of my ambitions or the accompanying isolation, stress, and loneliness?

Abraham's grandson's identity, like either Jason's, like so many, is bound up in grasping ambition. Jacob's grasping poisons every relationship in his life but one. It leads to profound isolation and is also a key part of his salvation. Looking into Jacob's story exposes the grabber within each of us. God's invitation through this story can transform us.

Jacob: What's in a Name?

Born a twin, Jacob and his brother, Esau, were both given literal, earthy names based on their physical appearance. Esau, the older brother, was born ruddy and covered in hair. His name means "hairy" or "rough." Jacob was born grasping his brother's heel and so was named "heel grabber."

Each of these names connotes far more than appearance however. One of the Hebrew roots of Esau's name is a verb meaning "to do" or "to make." Hebrew readers would associate Esau as a doer. The text of Genesis affirms this association: "When the boys grew up, Esau was a skillful hunter, a man of the field, while Jacob was a quiet man, living in tents" (Genesis 25:27). The name Esau both describes and characterizes the older twin. Contrasting Esau, the "man of the field," and Jacob, the "quiet man, living in tents" goes further. Esau is a make-stuff-happen kind of man. You almost expect the story to be about him.

Jacob, the heel grabber, is characterized in the next section of Scripture.

> Once when Jacob was cooking a stew, Esau came in from the field, and he was famished. Esau said to Jacob, "Let me eat some of that red stuff, for I am famished!" (Therefore, he was called Edom.) Jacob said, "First sell me your birthright." Esau said, "I am about to die; of what use is a birthright to me?" Jacob said, "Swear to me first." So he swore to him, and sold his birthright to Jacob. (Genesis 25:29-33)

Jacob grasps. In the ancient Near East the oldest son would inherit most of the family's wealth. Individualistic Western readers have trouble understanding this practice. Why not treat everyone equally? What Western readers fail to see is that the wealth of a family or clan did not belong to an individual but to the community. The patriarch was the leader of the family and steward of the resources. The oldest son was responsible to take on leadership of the family and stewardship of the family's property. This, in an age neither democratic nor individualistic, provided for the well-being of the whole community. When Genesis speaks of Esau's birthright, it means his place as inheritor of the family's wealth and leader of the family.

Read the scene again with these stakes in mind!

Jacob is subtle, perceptive, and ambitious. We're set up to see Esau as the doer, but Jacob flips a bowl of stew for the leadership of the family and control of its wealth. This not a fair trade. It's grasping, exploitative, and ruthless. This deal is so bad that even the text blames Esau for taking it (Genesis 25:34).

Jacob's characterization is complete. Jacob grasps. His name and character are one. Reading this story from the inside, I'm repulsed by Jacob. I want to see myself as generous, loving, and selfless. I judge Jacob for his selfishness. That is until I see a Jacob-like ambition reflected back in my own heart.

My first New York City apartment was on West 86th Street—two rooms facing a gray alley and a bathroom force fit between steam risers. The kitchen was as wide as the front door. Dishes overran the unusually deep sink on the day I moved in. The mound was still there the day I moved out. It was the pile of dishes that almost ended my friendship with Jason Raize before it began.

I hadn't been in the apartment one hour before mounting a full-scale assault on the dishes. Growing up, dishes were never allowed to linger in the sink. In high school I worked part-time as a dishwasher, spending the early morning hours rinsing, scrubbing, and stacking. These were just dishes, a call of duty. Jason, of course, was horrified. Who was this stranger in his apartment, invading his space, touching his things? We didn't speak much during the first two weeks we lived together.

Then, one day, something flipped. "You shaved!" Jason said brightly. My last job had been in a nineteenth-century living-history museum. I'd grown a beard for the character. "Yup," I said. And, just like that, we were friends.

After two weeks of living with Jason, I still wasn't sure what his name was. "Is your last name Rothenberg, or is it something else?" I asked, hesitantly. "Both," Jason said, as though the question didn't matter. "My family's name is Rothenberg," he said. "I'm Jason Raize."

Brian, the third roommate in our apartment, first interpreted Jason's name to me. I figured he'd adopted a professional name for the sake of convenience, just as I'd changed the pronunciation of my name ever since I started working. (My family's pronunciation was unintelligible to production assistants and stage managers who would call me into a room. After a while it just got easier not to correct them.) Brian corrected my perspective. "Raize is a mashup of two words." He said. "First is raise, with an *s* that means to lift up. The other, pronounced the same, but spelled with a *z* is raze, which means to demolish or burn down," he paused. "Jason is both. He's a rising star, and he'll demolish the barriers in his way."

Names are powerful.

Grasping for Blessing

Words are powerful. When our girls were small we used to have a weekly discipline of blessing one another. On Saturday evenings during dinner we would go around the table and bless one another. Hallie, the woman who taught us this practice, was careful to differentiate appreciation and blessing. "You appreciate someone for something they did or accomplished," she said. "I appreciate the way you cleaned your room or how you helped with the laundry," for example. "But," she continued, "you bless someone on the basis of who they are, their relationship to you, and who they are becoming, those qualities and characteristics that are shaping their future. I bless the ways you are growing in compassion, your giftedness in teaching, or your commitment to the truth," for example.

Those Saturday nights were powerful. The words of blessing we offered years ago linger today. The gifts that were named around the dining-room table—curiosity, compassion, confidence, and creativity—continue to shape the people who were blessed by them.

Jacob's story continues with a scheme to grasp not only his brother's birthright but also his blessing. Conspiring with his mother, Rebekah, Jacob impersonates his brother in order to receive his father's blessing. Why did Jacob grasp after his brother's blessing? Was Rebecca fearful that Jacob would miss out on something vital, something he'd need as he carried the family and covenant promises forward? Was Jacob afraid that somehow his grasping after his brother's birthright would be undone by Isaac's words?

Rabbi Jonathan Sacks points out that the blessing Isaac had prepared for Esau was different from the covenant blessing he had received from Abraham.

> He blessed Esau with the gifts he felt he would appreciate: wealth and power: "May G-d give you heaven's dew and earth's richness—an abundance of grain and new wine"— that is, wealth. "May nations serve you and peoples bow down to you. Be lord over your brothers, and may the sons of your mother bow down to you"—that is, power. These are *not* the covenantal blessings.

Jacob's grasping after this blessing has deep consequences. It ruins his relationship with his brother and grieves his father. Isaac "trembled violently" in distress when he discovers the deception (Genesis 27:33). Jacob's grasping threatens his life as his brother plots to murder him (Genesis 27:41).

Read the story imaginatively. Feel the betrayal. Look into the expressionless eyes of your father, the murderous hatred of your brother, and the conspiratorial gaze of your mother. The words of blessing feel so small. Was the cost was worth it?

I met Jason at the stage door after seeing him perform the role of Pontius Pilate in *Jesus Christ Superstar*. I heard him before I saw him. "Jason Gaboury!" he called out, voice booming above the crowd, pulling me into a hug. He had made it. "I can't believe you're touring with Ted Neely," I said. "Didn't he star in this movie before either of us were born?" Jason shrugged, "It's been great," he said.

My chest thumped in a way I desperately wanted to hide. He succeeded, at nineteen, to be on stage with stars. Jason managed to take a small but pivotal role and steal the show with it. Jason's

gospel vocal soulfulness, clarity, and flexibility was arresting. He sang like he was the son of Aretha Franklin and David Bowie trained by Freddie Mercury. "You reworked the arrangements," I said, shaking my head. "Wasn't all me," Jason shrugged, "but, yeah." "You're amazing," I said. I couldn't get the words "I'm so jealous" to come out. Why was that?

We stood together in the dim light. The awkward thumping returned. Jason went inside.

I'd driven several hours to see my friend, to celebrate his success, but the blessing I had for him stayed strangled in my chest. Why did Jason break through while I was doing a puppet show? Why did his vocal ability make me feel so small? Why couldn't I offer a blessing and affirm what was good, true, and beautiful about him?

That grasping ambition choked the joy out of a moment I'd never get back.

Gift in the Dark

Jacob's grasping ambition leads to his being sent away (Genesis 27:41–28:5). This is the first time Jacob's grasping isolates him from community. In contrast to his brother, a man of the field, we can assume Jacob, a man of the tents, is used to being with people, but his grasping has sent him into the wilderness alone. Jacob's blessing cost him the connections and relationships he was so keen to steward. I imagine Jacob walking north toward Haran knowing his twin brother wants him dead, each step feeling more and more like exile.

Alone at Bethel, Jacob is confronted by God for the first time. Curiously, God's presence does not come to Jacob in judgment of his grasping ways. God's presence does not come with a quest for Jacob to fulfill or a goal for him to achieve. Instead, God's presence comes to Jacob with a blessing and a gift.

The LORD stood beside him and said, "I am the LORD, the God of Abraham your father and the God of Isaac; the land on which you lie I will give to you and to your offspring; and your offspring shall be like the dust of the earth, and you shall spread abroad to the west and to the east and to the north and to the south; and all the families of the earth shall be blessed in you and in your offspring. Know that I am with you and will keep you wherever you go, and will bring you back to this land; for I will not leave you until I have done what I have promised you." (Genesis 28:13-15)

This is a significant moment. In these words, God gives to Jacob the covenantal promise he'd given to Abraham. Isaac's blessing, the one Jacob was so anxious to grasp for himself, was different. Jacob could not grasp for the covenant blessing of God. It is a free gift. God blesses Jacob at precisely the moment his grasping has isolated him and made him vulnerable.

Why would God give something so precious to a grabber like Jacob? Giving and grasping require the opposite motions of the finger and thumb. Grasping closes the fist into the shape of a paw. The hand loses its capacity to extend, explore, and caress. Giving opens the hand, releasing what it holds to another. Openhandedness builds relationship and extends trust.

God's generosity does not seem to have an immediate impact on the grabber. When Jacob wakes he's astounded by the presence of God, but rather than receive God's gift with trust and gratitude, Jacob tries to bargain and barter for it. He takes a vow:

If God will be with me, and will keep me in this way that I go, and will give me bread to eat and clothing to wear, so that I come again to my father's house in peace, then the LORD shall be my God, and this stone, which I have set up for a pillar, shall be God's house; and of all that you give me I will surely give one-tenth to you. (Genesis 28:20-22)

These are not the words of one receiving a gift but of a grabber trying to negotiate favorable terms. God did not ask for a tenth of Jacob's received gifts. In his promise God has already committed to be with Jacob and to bless him. There's no need for Jacob to grasp, and yet . . .

There was no need for Jason to grasp. His musical and theatrical gifts were so strong there was no question about his future on Broadway. Jason's posture toward his work was a sense of impenetrable confidence and unyielding pursuit. I couldn't help admiring his confidence or appreciating his talent, but getting to really know Jason was difficult.

One time Jason invited me to a piano bar to sing with him. I brought a piece I thought would be funny. The pianist played. I committed to the piece with all I had. It bombed. Jason felt embarrassed, not for me but for his reputation. He was fuming for a week, maybe more. It was as though my failure would somehow be contagious, that some guilt by association would undermine his aspirations.

What his fool of a friend had done was no liability to him. He didn't need to grasp.

Some time later, as we talked well into the morning, I caught a glimpse of the vulnerability underneath all that talent and confidence. Sitting together in a darkened living room, Jason shared his feelings of being misunderstood, his feelings of rejection from people he'd needed, and the fears of rejection as he worked through his sexual identity. It was the most honest conversation we ever had, a moment of deep connection. I imagined our friendship ripening to greater honesty, trust, and openness.

The next morning Jason's vulnerability had been replaced by his sideways grin and impenetrable confidence. There was no need for him to grasp, and yet . . . It was as if Jason's ambition and his vulnerability could not coexist.

Funhouse Mirror

They've recently repainted the play funhouses at the park. When our daughters were small we'd spend hours in this small space at the edge of Fort Tryon Park playing in the various spaces. Our girls loved the funhouse mirrors. "I'm taller than you!" one would shout, pointing at the elongated shape in the mirror. "Look how big my eyes are!" the other would say dreamily. We would laugh and explore.

Funhouse mirrors intrigue because of the way they exaggerate an image. Some features are brought near, others are pushed away. The mirror allows us to see in a fresh and often playful perspective.

Jacob's story continues in the home of his soon-to-be father-in-law, Laban. Laban's home is a funhouse mirror for Jacob the grabber, where his grasping ambition is reflected back to him in a fresh perspective. Jacob took advantage of Esau's appetite in order to take his birthright. Laban takes advantage of Jacob's sexual appetite, his love for his younger daughter. A bride price in the ancient world was not designed to be a way of enriching the father of the bride but was a way of demonstrating a groom had the means of providing for his family. Jacob was the heir of Isaac. He could have negotiated as a man of inheritance. But, anxious to grasp the beautiful woman he desires, Jacob makes a rash and unnecessary agreement.

At the wedding banquet, Jacob is deceived again. Laban gives his daughter Leah to Jacob rather than Rachel. Jacob does not see Leah until the morning after their wedding ceremony. Just as

Jacob had tricked his blind father, so now Laban has kept Jacob in the dark. We are meant to make a connection between Jacob grasping Esau's blessing and Laban deceiving Jacob with Leah. When an outraged Jacob confronts Laban, his father-in-law's cool reply, "This is not done in our country—giving the younger before the firstborn" (Genesis 29:26), is like a funhouse mirror, exaggerating Jacob's grasping attempts to supplant his brother.

Being on the receiving end of another's ambition does not immediately impact Jacob's grasping ambition. Instead, grasping ambition spreads. Jacob's wives grasp after his attention by competing with one another in how many children they could bring into the family. Laban continues to try to cheat Jacob and undermine his wages. Jacob continues to try to manipulate the flocks and herds so his wealth grows and his father-in-law's doesn't.

The grasping ambition poisons the whole family. As tensions escalate, Jacob flees from his father-in-law. He takes his wives, children, and livestock and sets off without a word. Once again, grasping ambition isolates Jacob and exposes him. Acquiring wives, children, and wealth did not bring security and a sense of well-being. It brought jealousy and made Jacob a target of others' ambitions.

"Are you going to be okay watching *Lion King* sweep?" Jean-Luc said as he came into the living room. Jean-Luc, a fellow campus minister, and I were sharing an apartment in Brooklyn. We'd just returned from two weeks of intensive ministry, and I'd crashed on the couch to watch the Tony Awards. "It's been a long week," he continued. "I know," I said. The voice on the television said, "And the winner is, *The Lion King.*"

"I'm happy for Jason," I said, unconvincingly. "I just wish that he was willing to talk to me." I remembered a few months earlier standing outside the stage door of the New Amsterdam Theatre on Broadway, just as I had when Jason was on tour. I wanted Jason to come outside, smile broadly, and shout to me across the crowd. I wanted to celebrate with him, to bless him. I sent a note backstage. Jason never came out.

"You've poured out a lot of energy this week," Jean-Luc continued. "There were some really powerful moments when you helped students meet God. It would be foolish to allow your sadness and jealousy of Jason Raize to steal the joy that comes from a week of significant ministry."

I switched the TV off.

It wasn't until years later that I wondered what this night was like for Jason. Who did Jason share this moment of fame and accomplishment with? Jason had accomplished his ambition. He had grasped the limelight. Was it satisfying, surreal, or hollow?

Not Letting Go: Jacob's Reshaped Legacy

Jacob's grasping has isolated him and exposed him to great risk. Laban pursues Jacob and catches up with him intending to bring him harm (Genesis 31:29). Jacob is powerless to protect himself, but God intervenes. It's as though Jacob is slowly beginning to recognize the generous activity of God. "If the God of my father, the God of Abraham and the Fear of Isaac, had not been on my side, surely now you would have sent me away empty-handed. God saw my affliction and the labor of my hands, and rebuked you last night," Jacob says (Genesis 31:42).

Jacob's transformation is even more apparent as he becomes a giver rather than a grabber. Jacob sends presents ahead to his brother, Esau. This turn of character is dramatic. Jacob's entire relationship with Esau has been characterized by grabbing and taking away what belongs to Esau. Now, Jacob initiates relationship through giving.

Jacob also prays differently. In the past Jacob's prayers have been transactional, "If you will bless me, then . . ." Now, Jacob prays,

> O God of my father Abraham and God of my father Isaac, O LORD who said to me, "Return to your country and to your kindred, and I will do you good," I am not worthy of the least of all the steadfast love and all the faithfulness that you have shown to your servant, for with only my staff I crossed this Jordan; and now I have become two companies. Deliver me, please, from the hand of my brother, from the hand of Esau, for I am afraid of him; he may come and kill us all, the mothers with the children. Yet you have said, "I will surely do you good, and make your offspring as the sand of the sea, which cannot be counted because of their number." (Genesis 32:9-12)

This prayer reflects a profound shift taking place in Jacob. Whereas he had been primarily concerned for himself, now he's deeply conscious of God's covenant blessing, God's direction, and God's provision. Jacob's grasping ambition is being reshaped by God's generosity.

Jacob's pivotal transformation happens that night. Alone by the stream of Jabbok, Jacob wrestles with a man all night long. It's a fascinating incident rich with interpretive possibilities. Jacob seems to be wrestling with a type of himself. The grabber is grabbed and vice versa. Yet Jacob recognizes this man as one who has the power to truly bless him. Jacob continues to grasp and grapple with all of his will, desperately refusing to let go even after sustaining a painful hip injury.

This incident brings Jacob to a brutal and transformative confrontation with himself and with God. Jacob's grasping ambition destroys his relationships, isolates him, and undermines his ability to represent the covenant God. Jacob's injury reminds him of his vulnerability and weakness. Jacob's willful clinging to this opponent changes his name and character. From that morning onward the grabber is called Israel, "the one who strives with God." Jacob describes the encounter as seeing God "face to face" (Genesis 32:30).

I imagine myself wrestling with a shadowy figure into the dawn. Only it's not my hip that gets injured but my voice. The instrument I use to persuade, influence, and lead is compromised permanently. I weep and don't let go. What blessing could possibly be worth the cost?

—————

"Are you sitting down?" Stuart asked. I thought he was going to tell me about a tragedy on campus. "What's going on?" I queried. "You didn't answer my question," Stuart said. "Okay. I'm sitting."

"Jason Raize is dead," Stuart said. "I read about it today and thought you'd want to know."

Jason's suicide, alone, on the other side of the globe, in anonymity, was the opposite of everything he'd been when I last saw him on television. I was so mad at myself for being jealous of him and so mad at him for not returning my note. I wanted to go back to that time backstage and give him the blessing that caught in my chest.

Jason's death forced me to rethink our relationship. His chosen name, his overwhelming confidence, his race to the top, as well as his descent into isolation, desolation, and despair became a funhouse mirror for me. Jason's ambition was externalized in performance, mine buried in jealousy, but both of us ended up lonely. As I enter into Jacob's story and reflect on Jason's story, trying to understand my own loneliness, I sense that grasping tendency in my own heart. I watch the way grasping poisoned the kind of connection and compassion real friendships need.

Would it be better not to be ambitious?

God's invitation to Jacob in his grasping ambition is not to become passive but to grasp and strive with God rather than against others. Jacob didn't need to grasp from his brother or father-in-law in order to receive the gift of God. He only needed to grasp the God who had chosen him. Jason didn't need to grasp a persona of impenetrable confidence in order to be the single greatest vocal talent in his field. It was a gift. Perhaps I don't need to grasp after activity, ministry success, or approval to receive the gift God has for me.

Grasping ambition isolates when that ambition is turned toward other people: their gifts, their abilities, their opportunities. What would it look like to bring our restless ambition to God and strive with God in prayer in those dark moments of self-doubt, in those moments of fear or envy? This question invites us out of loneliness, invites us to imagine becoming people whose ambitions and gifts serve others.

Jacob, as Israel, built a family that became a nation. His legacy remains with us. Ambitious and godly people have launched businesses, created art, led movements, invested resources, built communities, churches, and governments. Each ambitious woman or man can point to moments of isolation, loneliness, and challenge. Those who have moved from grasping to giving also point to moments or habits of wrestling truthfully and transparently with God. The healthiest learn to grasp God alone as the source of their well-being and anchor of their hope.

I wonder what Jason Raize's story might have been if he had learned to bring his restless ambition to God and confront the dark and vulnerable side he kept hidden.

Playing the cast album of *The Lion King*, I can still hear Jason's lament as he sings,

Home is an empty dream . . .
Father, I feel so alone.

The song ends in hope. A hope that I wish Jason had found.

> I know that the night must end . . .
> And I'll hear your voice deep inside.

It's not the best song on the album. Disney and Broadway are great at telling stories but are limited in their ability to engage human complexity. Still, I can't help longing for my friend to have wrestled with God even if he would've walked away with a limp.

For Reflection and Discussion

1. How would you describe your level of ambition? Do you long for greatness in your work, area of influence, or community?

2. In what ways has your ambition or tendency to grasp undermined relationships in your life?

3. What would it look like for you to bring your grasping ambition to God? How might doing so free you to serve others with your energy and gifts?

4. What descriptive name (for example, "grabber" or "doer") would best describe you at this moment? If God were to rename you, what name do you think God would choose?

5 | Listen

I rushed into our daughter's room at the sound of urgent tears. My then four-year-old was having a spiritual crisis. "Papa," she said. "I want to see Jesus. Why can't I see him? Why won't he come here?" she asked. Her vowels elongating on the *ee* sound, coming to an abrupt halt as sobs constricted her breathing, and then continuing a mournful staccato.

"It's okay, baby," I said gently, "did you have a bad dream?"

"No," she said, without any hint of consolation. "I was praying," she continued, "and asked Jesus to come and be with me in my room, but I can't see him. Why won't he come here?"

I felt my stomach tighten, the corners of my mouth turn down, and moisture pool in my eyes. *Stop that*, I thought. *You're no good to your daughter if you're crying too.*

Ronald Rolheiser describes my daughter's anguish as restlessness. "Restlessness is another type of loneliness," he writes, saying that it's about the "constant dissatisfaction" we feel.

> Our hearts and minds are so fashioned that they are never satisfied, always restless; never quiet, always wanting more of everything. . . . Religious thinkers have often called it "the spark of the divine to us"; philosophers sometimes

referred to it as "the desire of the part to return to the whole"; the Greeks had two names for it, *Nostos*, a certain home-sickness within the human heart, and *Eros*, a relentless erotic pull toward whatever we perceive as good; the Vikings called it "wanderlust," the constant urge to explore beyond all known horizons; . . . St. Augustine called it "rest-lessness." . . . Most of us simply call it "loneliness."

As a young teen, this same daughter was sitting in the living room with her middle school yearbook, looking over a particular set of photos. When I asked her what she was doing, she looked up, sighed, and said, "pining." We may not think of this persistent gnawing as loneliness, but its insatiable hunger draws us away, constantly away, from the present toward an unresolved future.

Seeking More of Everything

Our technology use accelerates this restlessness. The hunger for "more of everything," as Rolheiser wrote, is seductive and irre-sistible when we're connected by a pocket supercomputer to thou-sands of pictures and stories from everywhere on earth. These devices are addictive by design. In his summary of *Open to Persuasion*, a documentary about the social and psychological tools being manufactured into our devices, Canadian broadcaster Michael Enright writes, "Every ping, ding and vibration is de-signed with a purpose—to hook you, reel you in and keep you glued to your device for as long as possible. Is addiction inevitable?"

Social media accelerates this relational restlessness. Human beings like looking at one another. This practice of looking at an-other human being face to face begins just moments after we're born. Healthy babies enter a quiet alert state in which they are attentive to their environment. Contact with Mom or a caregiver prolongs this state in which the infant is "seeing" human faces for the first time. The wonder, attraction, and curiosity we experience simply looking at another person never go away. This is one of the reasons social media is so powerful. In it we see people and experience delight, curiosity, attraction, or envy. This dynamic of wonder and curiosity simply created by looking at other people is used to fuel in-person relationships.

"You play guitar!" Martin noticed. This simple observation led to a relationship that would change my life. How different this is from clicking a button or leaving a comment. No wonder loneliness is on the rise.

Social media redirects these impulses. Rather than looking at the person across the table, across the room, or across the counter, our curiosities are directed at people much farther away. When we put our smartphones down, though, we feel isolated. Instead of sharing the delight of the meal in front of us in real time with another person who can smell, taste, and share in the experience, we take pictures to share with an anonymous virtual crowd. Our curated images project the longings of who we wish we were and wall off the truth of who we are.

Restlessness points beyond our screens and social networks. In his book *Life After God*, Douglas Coupland's narrator describes himself as one of many who were "pushed to the edge of loneliness and who maybe fell off and who when we climbed back on, our world never looked the same." Coupland's prose is a white-knuckled effort to squeeze something ultimate, something satisfying, out of his experience. His book concludes with a confession.

Now—here is my secret:

I tell it to you with an openness of heart that I doubt I shall ever achieve again, so I pray that you are in a quiet room as you hear these words. My secret is that I need God— that I am sick and can no longer make it alone. I need God to help me give, because I no longer seem capable of giving;

to help me be kind, as I no longer seem capable of kindness;

to help me love, as I seem beyond being able to love.

Like my daughter calling out in the night, Coupland's narrator is restless and lonely.

Psalm 42 captures the restlessness and urgency of our experience.

As a deer longs for flowing streams,
    so my soul longs for you, O God. (Psalm 42:1)

Recently, while singing a popular worship chorus of this psalm, I was distracted by the disconnect. The music was a gentle series of arches. The congregation sang beatifically, as though the psalmist was describing a warm pastoral scene. But an animal longing or panting for water is not a graceful pastoral image. Imagine a deer staggering through an arid wasteland and pressing its tongue forward in an effort to moisten its mouth. Water is life in an arid climate. Death stalks the dehydrated. The psalmist's heart is panting after God, desperate to slake its thirst. The metaphor is stark. Here the desperation of a restless heart is on display. (In an attempt to resolve my inner dissonance between the psalm and song, I inserted a desperate panting noise into the verse. Sophia's horrified look ended that experiment.)

The next section of the psalm intensifies the loneliness and restlessness.

My soul thirsts for God,
    for the living God.
When shall I come and behold
    the face of God?
My tears have been my food
    day and night,

while people say to me continually,

"Where is your God?" (vv. 2-3)

The parallel structure of the poem connects the word *soul* with the word *tears*. The psalmist cries from the soul night and day without eating. When will God come? Where is he? These were my daughter's questions that night in bed, restless for companionship. They are the questions of every restless heart. These questions reveal the "quiet desperation" Thoreau said was the smoldering beneath even the "games and amusements of mankind."

Elijah's descent into loneliness and despair came after what we might expect to be his greatest victory. But instead of experiencing elation, joy, and celebration, Elijah finds himself running for his life, despondent, and lonely. God reveals himself to Elijah in the still, small, hidden voice. The call of God to Elijah and to us is to learn to listen.

Elijah: Listening for God's Voice

Elijah's name means "Yahweh is God." His name is a powerful characterization of who he is and what matters to him. Elijah appears suddenly in the fourth dynasty of the northern kingdom of Israel just as Baal worship is being introduced into the kingdom and promoted by the queen.

Described as "A fiercely Yahwist prophet in the tradition of Moses . . . appalled by the syncretism he encountered in Israel," Elijah rushes onto the scene with minimal introduction. He is a contrast to Ahab, the king of Israel, in every respect. Ahab is a cosmopolitan elite, the son of a king raised in the center of Israelite political power. Elijah is a rural character, with no pedigree, raised in a village so small and insignificant there's no other mention of it. Ahab is politically and religiously syncretistic. Elijah is a no-compromise prophet.

Elijah is all action. "Now Elijah the Tishbite, of Tishbe in Gilead, said to Ahab, 'As the LORD the God of Israel lives, before whom I stand, there shall be neither dew nor rain these years, except by my word'" (1 Kings 17:1). There is no call to repent, no appeal for a change in policy, no negotiation or compromise. After delivering this message of challenge to the king and to Baal, Elijah leaves the king and Israel to their fate.

When I was in Sunday school I thought Elijah was a biblical superhero—powerful, invulnerable to drought, and able to perform miracles. It seemed unfair that God selected some people for this kind of superhuman life. Now, of course, I realize I didn't understand the stories. They aren't really about Elijah but about a contest in the hearts of the Israelites between God and Baal. Elijah, a man of bold words and actions, has placed himself in the no-man's land between the reign of God and the claims of Baal.

A local Phoenician deity of storm and fertility, Baal was worshiped in order to ensure rain and a good harvest, the things that control life and death. Elijah's deeds and actions are designed to show the reader that Yahweh, not Baal, holds the keys of life and death, rain and harvest.

For example, when Elijah calls for a three-year drought, the Phoenician storm god is impotent to bring rain. While the people of the land scramble anxiously for food and water because of the drought, Elijah is settled by a pool of water. He doesn't hustle or fight to squeeze out a living but is instead cared for by the birds of the air (1 Kings 17:4-6). When the pool dries up, Elijah goes north into Sidon, the geographical territory of Baal. This is an inversion of the movement of Baal worship into Israel. As Elijah goes into Sidon, his first action is to sustain and then save the life of a widow and her son (1 Kings 17:9-16). Yahweh, the God of Israel, is not some tribal deity worried about his reputation. He is the true Lord of heaven and earth, the one who cares for widows and orphans. It's Yahweh, not Baal who can provide food, life, and sustenance.

The banter between Trevor Noah and his mother in his book *Born a Crime* captures the religious tension central to Elijah's story. Patricia, Trevor's mom, is a very devout woman whose life is organized around church. A typical Sunday involved going to three churches in three different communities. Trevor, by contrast, is a more independent thinker. He's skeptical about his mother's devotion. In the first chapter Trevor introduces us to this religious conflict, which will continue thematically throughout the book.

> Whenever I found myself up against my mother's faith-based obstinacy, I would try, as respectfully as possible, to counter with an opposing point of view.
>
> "Or," I said, "the Lord knows that today we *shouldn't* go to church, which is why he made sure the car wouldn't start, so that we stay home as a family and take a day of rest, because even the Lord rested."
>
> "Ah, that's the Devil talking, Trevor."

Trevor Noah's stories about growing up in a postapartheid South Africa regularly loop back to this religious conflict with his mom. Trevor Noah is rightly critical of Christianity as a tool of oppression and colonization. He gives voice to a postcolonial skepticism about Christian faith. His mom, by contrast, articulates the voice of a suprarational commitment to Jesus. Trevor's quick wit, narration, and skepticism carry most of the book, though never quite definitively closing down the tension.

At the end of the book, in an afterward without page numbers, Trevor Noah includes a story of one last argument with his mom. He'd introduced in the first chapter, in a passing comment that is highly foreshadowing, that his mom had been shot in the head. The book concludes with the story of his mom being shot, his rushing to the hospital and wrestling with his grief, anger, and potential financial ruin that paying for his mom's care might mean.

Inexplicably, the gun misfired four times while Noah's mom, Patricia, looked down the barrel and prayed. Only after the misfires, while attempting to run away, was she shot in the back of the head. Again, inexplicably, the bullet (though entering her head) missed all of the vital arteries and organs, including what appears to be a change in trajectory as the bullet was passing through her body.

Trevor Noah writes:

I was going on about how insane the whole week had been.

"You're lucky to be alive," I told her. "I still can't believe you didn't have any health insurance."

"Oh but I do have health insurance," she said.

"You do?"

"Yes. Jesus."

"Jesus?"

"Jesus."

"Jesus is your health insurance?"

"If God is for me, who can be against me?"

"Okay, mom."

"Trevor, I prayed. I told you I prayed. I don't pray for nothing."

"You know," I said, "for once I cannot argue with you. The gun, the bullets—I can't explain any of it. So, I'll give you that much." Then I couldn't resist teasing her with one last little jab. "But, where was your Jesus to pay your hospital bill, hmm? I know for a fact that He didn't pay that."

She smiled and said, "You're right. He didn't. But, He blessed me with the son who did."

The tension in the story of Elijah is the same as the conflict between Trevor Noah and his mother. Who or what is really in control of life and death? The answer to this primal question becomes the anchor of our inner restlessness. When we are restless for "more of everything," we, consciously or not, turn to whatever we believe to be in control of life and death. It could be God or Baal, Jesus or insurance, the right social network or the constant hustle.

Showdown: Elijah and the Prophets of Baal

After three years of drought, Elijah shows himself again to Ahab and invites a dramatic confrontation.

> When Ahab saw Elijah, Ahab said to him, "Is it you, you troubler of Israel?" He answered, "I have not troubled Israel; but you have, and your father's house, because you have forsaken the commandments of the LORD and followed the Baals. Now therefore have all Israel assemble for me at Mount Carmel, with the four hundred fifty prophets of Baal and the four hundred prophets of Asherah, who eat at Jezebel's table." (1 Kings 18:17-19)

Four hundred and fifty prophets of Baal versus one prophet of Yahweh. When the people and prophets assemble, Elijah challenges them to put their gods to the test. Whichever god hears the cries of the prophet(s) and sends fire to burn up the sacrifice deserves the people's loyalty. Everyone agrees.

The prophets of Baal waste no time in preparing the sacrifice. The prophets dance, wail, cut themselves, and carry on. Elijah mocks them. "Cry aloud! Surely he is a god; either he is meditating, or he has wandered away, or he is on a journey, or perhaps he is asleep and must be awakened" (v. 27).

Finally Elijah prepares an altar, arranges the sacrifice, and commands the sacrifice to be drenched with water twice. After calling on the Lord, fire comes down and consumes the soaked bull. The king and the people are astounded. The prophets of Baal are put to death. And in the real climax of the story, God sends rain upon the land.

Everything Elijah has been longing for has come true. Three years of drought are past. The king has seen the undisputable power of Yahweh. The prophets of Baal are destroyed. The people recognize that it's the Lord who sends the rain, who has power over life and death. As the rain pours down, Elijah, thrilled with the victory, races down the mountain ahead of Ahab and his chariots.

Elijah has faced overwhelming odds and succeeded, but all is not well. Contemporary American culture so loves the story of the individual hero beating the odds that we can't see the deep vulnerabilities within Elijah, who hasn't confronted his inner restlessness. He doesn't seem to be aware of his vulnerability to power, grandiosity, and self-pity. His heart is restless.

Lonely: Elijah's Desert Experience

Crowds are fickle. Elijah is still restless. Jezebel, the queen who introduced Baal worship, sends a message to Elijah threatening his life, and Elijah flees into the desert.

Why would a man who was willing to confront 450 prophets by himself suddenly flee in fear of a simple threat? It's as if all of Elijah's elation, all his confidence, and all his hopes for national repentance suddenly come crashing down around him in a single threat. This is out of character for a man whose ministry has been characterized by the power of God working in and through him.

Elijah flees into the wilderness and asks to die. "But he himself went a day's journey into the wilderness, and came and sat down under a solitary broom tree. He asked that he might die: 'It is enough; now, O Lord, take away my life, for I am no better than my ancestors'" (1 Kings 19:4). Elijah is not only scared, he's depressed. Elijah is despairing. His heart is sick.

We get the first glimpse of what is making Elijah's heart sick when he arrives at God's mountain.

> At that place he came to a cave and spent the night there.
>
> Then the word of the Lord came to him, saying, "What are you doing here, Elijah?" He answered, "I have been very zealous for the Lord, the God of hosts; for the Israelites have forsaken your covenant, thrown down your altars, and killed your prophets with the sword. I alone am left, and they are seeking my life, to take it away." (vv. 9-10)

Elijah's despair points to the loneliness and isolation he feels, "I alone am left." This isolation is brought about by his inner restlessness. It makes me wonder what Elijah expected to see happen after his victory on Mt. Carmel. Did he expect the king to renounce the queen? The king to enact some kind of sweeping legislation that would eliminate Baal worship from Israel forever? No resistance or setbacks? Instant cultural renewal? What was pounding in his heart that he couldn't see or articulate but nevertheless kept him up at night? Reading Elijah's story, I sense God asking me some tough questions. Did you expect ministry to resolve your sense of social isolation? Did you expect instant transformation? Are you even willing to name the restless pounding in your chest?

Picking up my daughter in the middle of the night stirs these questions. The desire to "just make it better" filled into my daughter's room casting a long shadow over our interaction. The loneliness, isolation, and grief that had sent me to Friar Ugo were now pounding in my chest. That restlessness for home, for health, for more of everything good wants to protect my daughter from her own experience. Both of us needed a word from God. Like Elijah, we needed to stop and listen.

Listen

Elijah's transformation in loneliness comes from encountering God in the sound of sheer silence. The word of the LORD said,

> "Go out and stand on the mountain before the LORD, for the LORD is about to pass by." Now there was a great wind, so strong that it was splitting mountains and breaking rocks in pieces before the LORD, but the LORD was not in the wind; and after the wind an earthquake, but the LORD was not in the earthquake; and after the earthquake a fire, but the LORD was not in the fire; and after the fire a sound of sheer silence. When Elijah heard it, he wrapped his face in his mantle and went out and stood at the entrance of the cave. (vv. 11-13)

Elijah's ministry had an unusually high amount of experiencing God in powerful signs and dramatic events. These experiences did not soothe the self-pity laden in Elijah's complaint. Knowing the power of God did not keep Elijah from despairing when his expectations weren't met. Elijah's powerful symbolic and authoritative actions did not enable him to see deeply into his own heart or empower him to trust in the slow work of God.

Listening to the sound of sheer silence, to the presence of God on the other side of the noisy world *out there* and the restless heart *in here* transforms Elijah forever. God's word, in sheer silence, redirects Elijah's ministry and perspective. He is to go and anoint a foreign king, a new king for Israel, and a new prophet. God's prophetic call to Israel was longer and more complex than Elijah understood. It wasn't to end gloriously on the mountaintop. God's call to Israel would echo through generations.

Like Elijah, we need to learn to listen to God in sheer silence

when our restlessness isolates and drives us toward despair. The Rule of St. Benedict, a tradition that has anchored Christian spirituality in the West for the last fifteen hundred years, begins with the word *listen*. "Listen carefully, my child, to my instructions, and attend to them with the ear of your heart. This is the advice from one who loves you; welcome it, and faithfully put it into practice." The call of this loving guide is to listen well and deeply, not simply to a set of rules and instructions for religious life but to the voice of God. Joan Chittister writes, "Benedictine spirituality forms us to listen always for the voice of God. When my own noise is what drowns that word out, the spiritual life becomes a sham. . . . Make no doubt about it, the ability to listen to another, to sit silently in the presence of God, to give sober heed, and to ponder is the nucleus of Benedictine spirituality."

I lifted my daughter out of her bed. Her body stiffened as I curled her toward me and then went limp as I held her to my chest. Her breath was still stuttering with her last sobs. "Come sit with me," I said, as we made our way to the rocking chair, each breath a silent petition, "Lord, speak to our restless hearts."

"Let's just listen for a while," I said settling into the chair. Slowly, her breathing settled down. After we'd been quiet for a while I asked, "Do you know how to look for Jesus?" She looked puzzled. "Maybe Jesus wants to teach you how to look for him in the places he promised he'd always be," I continued. "Where?" she said curiously. "Well, Jesus said he'd be there when we read Scripture. Did we do that tonight?" She nodded. "Jesus said he'd be there when we come around the Communion table at church. Maybe we can look for him there." She nodded. "And," I continued, "Jesus said he'd be there inside other people who know and love him." Her weight shifted back as she yawned. "So, maybe being here together is a way we can see Jesus." She began to settle. "I still want to play with him," she said. "Me too!" I said. "Maybe we can play together tomorrow and think about ways Jesus is with us." We sat quietly for another few minutes before I carried her back to bed.

Listening to God in silence creates the perspective needed to differentiate between my woundedness or drive and the needs of the people around me. When I listen past my need to "make it better" to the sheer silence of God, it creates an anchor for my restlessness and helps me to love well.

For Reflection and Discussion

1. How have you experienced restlessness? In what ways has it contributed to your sense of isolation and loneliness?

2. Where have you experienced God's generosity, power, and provision in your life? How have those moments shaped your perspective of God?

3. What's your experience with listening to God in solitude and silence? What would it take to integrate five minutes of solitude or silence into your daily or weekly rhythms?

4. Who in your life practices listening in solitude and silence? What about their life with God is attractive to you? What might you be able to learn from them?

6 | Grieve

I was in fourth grade when my mom moved out. Mom and Dad's relationship had been characterized by tension and fighting for a year by then. One day a twin bed showed up in what, till that point, had been the dining room. "Dad's sleeping there," my sister said. Neither of us ever saw him in it.

Of all the families we knew, most of them through church, there were no people more committed to Jesus than our parents. Mom had stitched and cross-stitched the kneeler pillows our parish used every week at Communion. She'd created religious banners for the sides of the sanctuary. She sewed vestments for lay readers, acolytes, and choir members. Mom attended morning prayer every weekday, attended Bible study on Tuesday mornings, led a prayer group on Friday nights, sang in the choir, and threw herself into every holiday, special service, and bake sale. (One time she made so much fudge for a church event that even after giving pounds of it away we still had fudge in the freezer for years to come.)

Dad was just as committed. He sang in the choir, served as a lay reader, and served multiple terms as the church warden—the layperson responsible for the church buildings, budget, and physical needs of the congregation. When our little parish needed a building to connect the small, early twentieth-century parish house and the small, mid-twentieth-century sanctuary, Dad built it. He oversaw the project and did much of the framing and construction himself.

As a kid, I didn't understand grown-up relationships. I understood that Jesus wanted families to be loving communities where parents and children felt safe. I understood that my parents loved Jesus. I couldn't understand why Jesus couldn't just make my parents love each other. If any couple deserved a miraculous intervention, it seemed they should be on the top of the list.

When you're a kid and you have a fight with your brother or sister, an intervening parent sends everyone to a corner or room to cool off and then brings the siblings back together and says, "Okay, what happened?" Each child gets to tell his or her version of the story. Meanwhile, the parent reminds children of the rules that were violated. "So, you took your brother's toy away from him while he was playing with it?" "Yes, but . . ." "We don't take things from each other without asking, do we?" "No," says the child. The parent continues, "So, you didn't respond to your brother when he asked you to share?" "Yes, but . . ." "We share in our family." There's a sigh. "Okay." Then there's an apology, sometimes even a forced hug, and the conflict is over. I kept wondering, *Why doesn't Jesus just make Mom and Dad apologize to each other, hug, and then we can be a loving family again?*

The night my mom left was the most frightening, violent, and chaotic I'd ever seen between them. My older sister and younger brother and I took refuge in the basement while banging and raised voices gathered momentum above us. The crash of a pot on the stove. Dad's voice. Mom's voice. Stomping feet. Thump . . . rumble . . . throaty shouting. We huddled together under a knitted afghan. "Dear Jesus, please make them stop." Bang. "Jesus,

"Jesus . . . please."

Jesus didn't come. When quiet finally came, we crept up the stairs and discovered that Mom was leaving. Our family, as we'd known it, died.

Ezekiel: Denying Death

I hate death. I bet you do too, whether it comes after a long illness, an icy stillness, or crushed willfulness. We hate the finality of it, the banality of it, and the violence of it. We hate the death of our loved ones, the death of close relationships, the death of our dreams, the death of our faculties, the death of opportunity, and the death of community. And we hate that *everything dies*.

Death is the ultimate isolation. Death separates us from the person, the ideal, the opportunity we held dear. In this separation it's as if a part of us dies as well. Some of the hooks we used to hang our sense of identity on are bent out of shape; others are missing entirely. Who am I when my dream of marriage dies in midlife? Who am I when I'm cut off or estranged from parents, siblings, or my faith community? Who am I when I fail? Who am I when my career ambitions die, when I'm out of work, or when I just can't reach my teenage son or daughter?

In contemporary Western culture, we usually deal with death in one of two ways: denial or despair. Both further isolate us and increase loneliness. God's invitation draws us into the tempest of anger, sadness, doubt, and emptiness. If we're willing to walk into that terrifying and chaotic swirl of emotion, we can discover death-defying hope.

Our cultural moment most often deals with death by denying it. We eat acai berry and kale salad to supercharge our bodies. Whole industries have developed promising to help us look and feel younger. We have assisted-living facilities where we can isolate those whose health is failing and insulate ourselves from confronting our mortality. We experience compassion in the wake of the great tragedies of our day—death and displacement in Syria, famine in East Africa, the crisis in Yemen—but quickly move on.

The desire to deny death is older than we imagine. In 607 BC the kingdom of Judah and the city of Jerusalem were taken captive by the Babylonian Empire. The Judean king, Jehoiachin, was carried off into Babylon, with a puppet king, Zedekiah, installed in his place. The fall of Jerusalem was an encounter with death at multiple levels. Families had been decimated by starvation and war. The city's walls, its only real defenses, were breached. Solomon's temple still stood but was vulnerable. Judah's cultural leaders were taken away to Babylon. These events, while tragic, were only the beginning of Jerusalem's destruction and exile. Jeremiah rightly prophesied about the defeat of Jerusalem but had also warned that the whole city would be desolate and the temple destroyed (Jeremiah 26:1-12).

What do you do when you've lived through the trauma of war and are still vulnerable? What do you do when you're under pressure to conform to political leadership that is culturally dissonant? How do you deal with the vulnerability that comes from knowing more devastation may be on the way? These questions have painful contemporary relevance even though they originate in ancient history.

Ezekiel tells about a group of people committed to dealing with this spiritual, cultural, and physical death by denying it. They are called false prophets. This particular group preached during a period between Jerusalem's first defeat by the Babylonians and the ultimate destruction and devastation of Jerusalem and of Solomon's temple in 587 BC. These prophets were saying, in essence, "Jerusalem will not be utterly destroyed. Everything is fine. Our defeat by Babylon was just a minor setback. Don't worry; be happy" (Ezekiel 13:10).

These false prophets embody something Western culture has come to expect with religious people: denial. Marx argued that "Religion is the sigh of the oppressed creature, the heart of a heartless world, and the soul of soulless conditions. It is the *opium* of the people." Marx's point was that religion was understandable only as an escapist fantasy. The promise of reward in heaven is nothing more than a form of social control designed to keep human beings from confronting the reality of their oppression. Liberation from religion would, Marx believed, lead to human flourishing.

Marx's ideas continue to influence contemporary culture, though they often aren't directly attributed to him. According to David Kinnaman's research, young people are leaving the church in large numbers because of their experience and perception that the church is overprotective, shallow, antiscience, repressive, exclusive, and doubtless. What do these criticisms have in common? Underneath each is an assumption that life, from science to morality to cultural engagement to epistemology, is more complicated than our Christian practice is willing to engage. The perceived response to this complexity is denial. But, far from resolving contemporary challenges, this denial simply makes Christian faith less plausible to young people. This expression of Christian faith is the "soul of soulless conditions," a flight from honest engagement with death in its intellectual, cultural, social, and moral forms.

Scripture does not avoid complexity or death. Ezekiel confronts the false prophets with the sober reality, saying, "Thus says the Lord GOD, Alas for the senseless prophets who follow their own spirit, and have seen nothing! Your prophets have been like jackals among ruins, O Israel" (Ezekiel 13:3-4).

Denial as Collusion

Denial does not resolve the trauma, isolation, and vulnerability we experience in death. On the contrary, when we deny death, we end up colluding with it.

The musical *Dear Evan Hansen* is fueled by conflict created by death and denial. We are introduced to Evan as a socially anxious young man with a broken arm. Evan's therapeutic practice of writing letters to himself in order to "build his confidence" doesn't seem to be working.

Evan's main desire is to be seen, to be noticed, to matter.

On the outside, always looking in
Will I ever be more than I've always been? . . .
Waving through a window, oh
Can anybody see, is anybody waving back at me?

His isolation and sense of disconnection from others is profound. It leads him to lie. Evan creates a pretend relationship with a student who had recently committed suicide as a way to avoid or deny his own sense of social isolation and the ways it has caused him to flirt with death.

Evan's lies seem to give him what he wants. He is noticed. He's embraced by a family system he's never had. He starts a romantic relationship he's pined for. Evan moves from isolation and anxiety to being internet famous. And yet the more Evan lies, the more he becomes estranged from his mother and the friends he had at the start. Denial and fantasy become more and more deadly to Evan's well-being.

The climax of the musical is when Evan decides to tell the truth. He sings,

What if everyone knew?
Would they like what they saw?

Or would they hate it too?

Will I just keep on running away from what's true?

This confession shatters the illusion Evan has created. It's also the beginning of Evan's restoration. In the wake of Evan's stepping into truth, we discover parts of Evan's story that have been hidden. We learn, for example, that Evan's broken arm is the result of a failed suicide attempt. We learn the story of Evan's grief and anxiety over his dad's leaving him and his mom fourteen years earlier.

These discoveries reframe the story. A story that has, so far, been about managing self and social perception but becomes a story of deferred grief. As long as Evan is denying death, his own flirtation with it, the death of his relationship with his father, and the truth of his fellow student's death, he's unable to build the kind of connections he desperately wants. His denials collude with death, isolating him, increasing his loneliness.

Evan Hansen needs to grieve, to enter into the painful truth in order to become free.

We hate the way death creeps into our lives, churches, relationships, and calling. It's so tempting to deny it, to pretend it doesn't matter, but we can't. We can't deny it because when we deny death we simply collude with it.

The Language of Despair

Another way we deal with the reality of death is by giving in to despair. We see evidence of despair in the book of Ezekiel as well, especially in chapter 37 on the valley of dry bones. The setting of this passage is after the destruction of Jerusalem and the temple in 587 BC. There's no more false hope. "Our bones are dried up, and our hope is lost; we are cut off completely" (Ezekiel 37:11). This is the language of despair.

Ezekiel is not shielded from despair. Describing his experience in the valley of dry bones, Ezekiel says, "He led me all around them; there were very many lying in the valley, and they were very dry. He said to me, 'Mortal, can these bones live?' I answered, 'O Lord GOD, you know'" (Ezekiel 37:2-3). It's possible to read this response as pious deference, but the imagery of the text leans away from such a reading. After the razing of Jerusalem, Ezekiel finds himself in a valley of death. Bones picked clean by carrion and baked by the sun surround him on every side. These bones are the empty remnants of what was once life. They are a visceral and visual reminder of what has happened to Judah politically and culturally. In this context, Ezekiel's answer takes on a despairing tone. Death is final; death is all around him. By saying, "God only knows," Ezekiel gives voice to despair.

Ezekiel isn't alone. Despair says, "What's the point of reaching out to that relative, colleague, friend, or broken relationship? Things will never change." Despair says, "I'm too old; time and opportunity have passed me by." Despair says, "It's too broken, too far gone, too difficult."

We see the fingerprints of despair in the New Testament as well. In John 11, after the death of Mary and Martha's brother, Lazarus, they both greet Jesus with exactly the same words: "Lord, if you had been here, my brother would not have died" (John 11:21, 32). These sisters seem to assume that Jesus could have intervened and healed Lazarus, but now there's nothing but the stench of death.

The lingering stench of death isn't just physical. It can be relational. You can see it in the hopelessness that lingers after death or disillusionment. Once on campus, I asked Sarah a question I often ask students: "If God were standing in front of you, what would

you ask him?" She became deadly serious. "I'd ask him about my
mom," she said. "What is it about your mom?" I asked. Sarah
shared that she'd watched her mom, diagnosed with ALS when
Sarah was in middle school, transition from being a strong, independent woman to someone who needed to be fed and washed.
Sarah began to weep as she described the disease taking away her
mom's ability to speak or write.

It was well past time, from Sarah's perspective, for God to have
done something to help her mom. Sarah waited for her mom's
death with strength and courage on the outside while despair and
resignation gnawed at her from within.

There is profound loneliness in despair. "I don't understand
what's happening," Sarah said through sobs, "I never cry like this."

Have you ever had grief so deep you couldn't capture it in
words, even to yourself? Imagine you're Ezekiel walking through
a mass grave, contemplating the destruction of your people and
culture. Listen to the voice of God asking, "Can these bones live?"
What arises in response? Imagine your beloved brother has died
after you've reached out to Jesus for help, but Jesus didn't come.
Imagine Jesus showing up at the funeral. What do you want to
say to him?

When we were growing up, we used to have a poster in the
hallway by our bedrooms of Jesus blessing the little children. Jesus
smiles brightly, arms extended. Children smile back. I used to
look at that poster for comfort and reassurance. Smiling Jesus was
there when I had a bad dream or was in bed with chills and a fever.
The night Mom left, smiling Jesus had no comfort. Had the poster
been faded and curling before? How hadn't I noticed?

I've often imagined Jesus showing up at my house after Mom
left. My response to Jesus is the same as that of Mary and Martha,
"Jesus, where were you? Why didn't you answer? How could you
just leave us frightened and alone?"

This despair is a direct assault on the character and capacity of God. In the face of death or loss we feel abandoned by God; we feel as if God doesn't care or perhaps is powerless to bring change.

The gospel has good news for Israel in exile, Mary and Martha in grief, Sarah in her pain, and you and me in our powerlessness. It's an invitation to grieve. Left unexpressed and unexplored, despair will poison any sense of intimacy and connection with God. While an invitation to grieve doesn't intuitively sound like good news, it's actually the only way to discover hope.

Grief and Hope

God does not leave us powerless or isolated. The gospel enables us not to deny or to despair because of death but beckons us to death-defying hope. To pursue this hope God invites us to grieve in his presence. Walking through grief is scary. Entering into the Scriptures to grieve alongside or in the presence of God can transform us deeply.

"When Jesus saw her weeping, and the Jews who came with her also weeping, he was greatly disturbed in spirit and deeply moved. He said, 'Where have you laid him?' They said to him, 'Lord, come and see.'" This passage leads to the shortest and most pointed verse in the New Testament, "Jesus began to weep" (John 11:33-35). In Greek, the sentence is two words and a definite article. John places the verb *dakryō* first, to emphasize the action. The sentence reads not *Jesus* began to weep (emphasis on Jesus) but Jesus *began to weep* (emphasis on weep). Earlier references to weeping in John 11 use a different verb, *klaiō*. The change in verb as well as word order amplifies John's message. The tears Jesus shed at the tomb of his friend stick in minds and imaginations.

Enter into this scene. Can you imagine Jesus' eyes welling up with tears? Can you see the sorrow as his shoulders slump forward, jerking up and down as he allows himself to weep?

What difference does it make that Jesus weeps in the face of death? And if *he* does, who are we to deny death? Jesus' tears bring the divine Word of John 1 into direct contact with the relentless sorrow, emptiness, and chaos of death in our world. Because Jesus grieved alongside Mary, we can have confidence that Jesus weeps along with us as we confront death.

Jesus' tears are not simply an exercise in empathy with Mary, but they also witness to the character of Jesus' relationship with Lazarus. Verse 36 says, "So the Jews said, 'See how he loved him!'" Jesus' tears express wordlessly his love and commitment to Lazarus. Jesus did not abandon his friend or forget his profound need. Jesus loved Lazarus deeply. Tears are the expression of love in the face of death.

Entering into this Scripture, I discovered that beneath the sense of isolation and loneliness I'd gone to Friar Ugo to resolve was a well of unresolved grief. I imagine myself in the Scriptures with Mary and Martha, but the setting is not first-century Palestine but twentieth-century western Massachusetts.

Jesus walks into my room after Mom had left. What do his tears mean? Are they tears of pity on a group of hurt and frightened kids or something more profound? As I sit with Jesus in the story of Mary, Martha, and Lazarus, I see him weep for my mom and dad as their words and actions wound one another deeply. I see him weep for children scared and scarred. I see fierce commitment to love beyond trauma, divorce, and even death.

Sitting with Jesus in this space frees my own tears. Years of resignation give way revealing a tempest of rage, fear, bitterness, and sadness. I weep. Jesus weeps. As we weep together, it's unclear who's weeping with and for whom. Jesus' tears express my sorrow and rage. My tears express his tenderness toward Mom and Dad. In the midst of loneliness, as I observe my parents' marriage die and grieve for the loss of our family, I find myself grieving with Jesus. His grief expands mine, reforging connections between us.

Entering into this grief with Jesus doesn't undo the tragedy of death. My parents' separation and divorce had a lasting impact. But the isolation, fear, and sadness of this experience are transformed. The loneliness of death is somehow transformed, not through a change of circumstances but through an emotional connection with God in the midst of grief. Inside the well of grief there's a new current strangely like hope.

Both Ezekiel 37 and John 11 inspire hope. As a prophet or sisters grieve in the presence of God, they experience God's power over death. It is not simply that God empathizes with us in our grief, God holds the power of life and death in his hands. Ezekiel's answer, "O Lord God, you know," captures the emotional realism of a man on the brink of despair, but it's also a statement of faith. We may struggle to articulate faith when we feel overwhelmed by sadness, anger, or fear, but biblical writers do it all the time. "Out of the depths I cry to you, O Lord" (Psalm 130:1).

Praying along with Mary and Martha, "Lord, if you had been here . . ." enables us to turn grief into prayer. "So, where the hell are you, God?" is not a failure in piety or faith. It's the prayer of a mom in anguish grieving over a change in her relationship with her son that feels like death. Janice prayed these words with me recently. They were an expression of what she described as heartbreak. "I stand with one foot in deeply accessible joy, knowing God's love. My same body holding devastation and comfort."

Entering God's Word having read, marked, learned, and inwardly digested it enables hope. God was at work in the exile. Jesus wept at Lazarus's tomb. We can have hope in the present because God has revealed himself in the past.

Both the Ezekiel and John texts also point to resurrection—the promise of God for the people of God. A "sure and certain hope of the resurrection to eternal life," as one prayer book put it, is not a denial of the pain and loss of death. It is the confidence in a transformed and continuous existence and longing for that place where there is neither death nor suffering.

I need the hope of the resurrection not just to lighten the load of past grief but also to negotiate relationships in the present. When Sophia and I are struggling to communicate and it's tempting to shut down emotionally, the resurrection of Jesus means that there is a power in the gospel stronger than the death of my parents' marriage I experienced as a child. When a relationship gets difficult, the resurrection energizes me to face the truth instead of trying to protect myself. The pain and death of our family structure don't get to determine our options and dominate the future. There is a power bigger than death.

Notice the way Jesus makes God's life available to us. In John 11 Jesus calls Lazarus out of the tomb. But this isn't the end of the story. Jesus is not simply calling Lazarus to life; he is initiating the chain of events that will bring about his own death. Lazarus comes out of the tomb—Jesus is headed into the tomb.

In Jesus the very life of God was poured out to death, which means there is no place, not even death, where we cannot meet the life of God. Denial and despair hold us back from the gift of God in the midst of death, Jesus himself. Stepping into grief with Jesus enables us to hope.

For Reflection and Discussion

1. Where in your life have you experienced isolation and desolation as a result of death? (Include the death of relationships, hopes, expectations, etc.)

2. Are you more tempted to deny death or get caught in despair? How do these strategies isolate you?

3. Enter into the Ezekiel and John passages imaginatively. What comes up for you emotionally as you bring your grief to God?

4. How might Jesus be inviting you to hope?

7 | Risk

How does activism get lonely?" I asked my friend Jonathan Walton.

His deep exhale was a sigh, chuckle, and groan all at once. This is a sound I've come to associate with Jonathan when he's under pressure. I've heard it a lot since the death of Michael Brown in 2014. The following piece is part of Jonathan's answer:

> I am an Ivy League educated black male and know what it's like to put on a hoody and be rendered invisible to my white and Asian classmates. I also know what it's like to think that an elite education, the right clothes, and good English will somehow lighten the burden of blackness and lift the implicit bias and alleviate the fear of black men perpetuated by television, media, music, and kitchen table conversations between parents and children for generations. . . .
>
> I began to feel small, powerless and hopelessly outnumbered as it seems I'll never be able to cry loud enough or long enough for white people, immigrants, and some other black Americans to think my sadness is their problem. Small, because black men like me are only 6 percent of the U.S. population but 40 percent of all homicides. Selah. Powerless because the average net worth of Congressional members is

$1,066,500 and the average net worth of black Americans is $4,900. And hopelessly outnumbered because more people are willing to allow harsh sentences to be passed down for black males when their white counterparts go free and the Voting Rights Act is systematically rolled back than those willing to march, petition or vote for fairness.

These and more thoughts were coursing through my brain when my wife wrapped her arms around me and leaned in for a kiss; and I told her to "leave me alone." My beautiful, empathetic, caring wife who wants to affirm my worth and identity, longs to see the image of God affirmed in everyone and works tirelessly for justice and opportunity in black, brown and immigrant communities—I pushed her away.

Deeply hurt, she went to bed and I got my wish. I was alone. Score another victory for racism.

Jonathan's words articulate multiple points of isolation and loneliness. There is the pain of identification with acts of violence against black men. There is the isolating pain of disillusionment as the structures of the academy, ability, and approachability do not protect a young man like Jonathan from being held at gunpoint by police. There is a sense of loneliness that comes from a history of injustice as well as a sense of disconnection that no one cares.

Choosing to raise your voice in the face of injustice intensifies these vulnerabilities. What if your words are misunderstood? What if your words or actions upset the people you're close to? These outcomes are not just possible but likely.

In their book *Loneliness: Human Nature and the Need for Social Connection*, John Cacioppo and William Patrick argue, "Loneliness rarely travels alone." Depression, anxiety, hostility, and sadness are all distinct emotional states but are strongly influenced by loneliness. Compelled by loneliness to reach out for

change, Jonathan is also experiencing fear of rejection, appropriate hostility toward injustice, dejection, and grief. Each of these emotions reduces our capacity to accurately interpret the messages of other people and to control our response. The poignant moment at the end of the previous quote, Jonathan rejecting his wife's affections, is an example of compound emotions shutting down the ability to connect and communicate, the one thing so desperately needed.

Social Media and Loneliness

It's tempting to imagine that the broader and more intentionally curated context for activism through new media might make it easier to stay emotionally connected while engaging in activism.

According to Pew research, 53 percent of all Americans have been involved in some kind of online civil activism within the last year, while over 65 percent believe that social media is important for getting politicians to pay attention to issues and creating social movements. Around the United States and around the world, we're spending more time online. That online presence and participation have a socially active edge. It's worth asking whether this civil activism is helping us be more civil or more active.

The initial evidence isn't good. In his book *Lost Connections*, Johann Hari writes, "The internet was born into a world where many people had already lost their sense of connection to each other. . . . The web arrived offering them a kind of parody of what they were losing—Facebook friends in place of neighborhoods, video games in place of meaningful work, status updates in place of status in the world." Whatever causal relationship social media has to our sense of isolation and loneliness, it is unable to provide the in-person contact and connections we need to thrive.

What does our increased engagement in civil activism and decline in the sense of connection to one another mean? How might these trends relate to one another?

One thing's for sure, we are increasingly isolated. Our tastes, habits, interests, education, and income are being tracked in order to persuade us to buy the next gadget, click on the next video, and consume the next experience. Marilyn McEntyre reflects, "When even our babies are a target market, and armies of young professionals are taking careful aim, it's time to recognize that there's something lurking in the big-box stores that's worth resisting."

The combination of declining personal connections, constant marketing bombardment, and the promise of new media offering a parody of what we've lost could account for the context we find ourselves in. We are more civically minded and less civil. We are more inclined toward activism and less active in churches, community groups, and neighborhood associations. As we continued talking, Jonathan said, "What happens when I post or protest is that I feel seen, valued, celebrated, and included. These feelings don't last though because they're not anchored in something permanent. The protest will end. The hashtag will fade."

Jonathan's story of encountering loneliness and isolation is different from the one that launched me on a spiritual quest to understand loneliness in Scripture, but there are overlapping themes. Jonathan, too, is a campus ministry leader and activist in his thirties. His life is full of people, activity, and even meaningful relationships. And yet his loneliness speaks to me of our shared need to discover friendship with God in Scripture and in practice.

The longing for a better, more just, and healthier world is an important part of our shared humanity. The amplifying power of our communication technologies means more and more of us can be informed and engaged with this vital part of our humanity.

These technologies do not minimize the risks of activism, nor do they make us less lonely.

Distinct loneliness accompanies risk. Activists and artists know this kind of isolation and the loneliness that accompanies the vulnerable work they immerse themselves in. As more of us engage in civil activism in-person or online, we will experience an increase in loneliness. Esther's story can help us anchor the invitation to risk for the sake of others in the character of God and the complexities of our broken world.

Esther: Justice and Vulnerability

Excess and injustice create the context and conflict for the story of Esther. The book opens in the palace of Ahasuerus (also called Xerxes) king of Persia. The king is throwing a party. Actually, the king is throwing an after-party. The first of his parties lasted six months. During this party, the king "displayed the great wealth of his kingdom and the splendor and pomp of his majesty for many days" (Esther 1:4). After this party ended, the king threw a smaller party, just for the people in the citadel of Susa, and included wine "without restraint" (v. 8).

The opulence of these parties is only possible because of the unchallenged success of the Persian Empire's conquest and subjugation of nations and peoples. The king was said to "rule over" 127 provinces from India to Africa.

The purpose of this six-month party and week-long after-party is to showcase the king's wealth and invulnerability. The message is clear: the king has unimaginable wealth and power and can bestow wealth, honor, and power on the ones he chooses. Do right by the king (support his rule and dominion), and some of this great wealth and power may rub off on you. Cross the king, and you are assured annihilation.

Debra Reid argues that this context is crucial for under-standing Esther.

> Esther finds its meaning within such a setting. It concerns the fate of a group of Jews, who, about fifty or sixty years after being allowed to return to Jerusalem, still found them-selves in the eastern Persian Empire. Their situation was not easy. . . . This volatile situation lies behind the drama of the Esther story—for its first readers the tension would need no explanation. To this, the religious tension needs to be added. We know that Xerxes completed the palace at Persepolis, in honor of himself and the Zoroastrian god Ahuramazda. . . . To a king who made religious concerns his business, the Jewish population with their own religion and customs would be viewed as particularly troublesome.

If we are right to view Esther's story through the lens of activism, it's important not to lose sight of the categorical vulnerability of the people of God. The particularities of Esther's position, gender, shrewdness, and her uncle Mordecai add dramatic tension to an already explosive context.

As the crowning finale of king Ahasuerus's after-party, he com-mands Vashti, the queen, to display her beauty and stature before his guests. In summoning Vashti as an object in which to display his power and status, the king exploits marriage as a structure of domination. The queen is expected to simply obey her husband's demands, just like everyone else. But in this first reversal in a book full of dramatic reversals, Vashti refuses.

Vashti's refusal is what a dramatist calls *the inciting incident*, the conflict or event that sets the main plot of the story in motion. Hamlet deciding to keep watch for his father's ghost, Hagrid breaking down the door on Harry's eleventh birthday, and Rachel Chiu agreeing to visit Nick Young's family in Singapore are all inciting incidents. These incidents tell the readers or audience members what the story is about and where the main conflict lies: vengeance for a father's murder, a secret wizarding world with the clues to open up a young boy's past and future destiny, an impossibly rich and elitist family that Rachel may never measure up to. This inciting incident tells us that the book of Esther is about a woman willing to challenge an opulent, self-indulgent, impulsive, and power-intoxicated king.

Queen Vashti's no is a powerful and resonant statement for our own time. #MeToo and #ChurchToo movements have brought fresh light to the scope and problem of sexual harassment in entertainment, finance, the church, and politics. The strength of these movements may be described as powerful nos to the social pressure to stay silent about sexual harassment.

> Confronted by sexism like that of Xerxes, women have a number of possible reactions open to them. . . . [One] is simply to say "No"; that is what Vashti does. . . . [O]ne might picture these as choices, as if a woman decides which kind of woman to be, but I am not sure this is really the dynamic of what happens. I doubt if Vashti has much choice. She does what she has to do in order to be her own person and be able to look at herself in the mirror, even though the price she pays is being deposed from her position as queen and wife.

The isolation Vashti experiences because of her no should not be minimized. The temptation to vilify those who challenge assumptions and power dynamics is powerful. Her no cost her. The king's sycophantic advisers recommend "that Vashti is never again to come before King Ahasuerus; and let the king give her royal position to another who is better than she" (Esther 1:19). Blamed as not good enough, Vashti bears public and legal scorn for her simple act of defiance. We are to read the rest of the book aware not only of the precarious position of the Jews but also of the risks a woman opens herself to when she challenges the king.

After Vashti's deposition, the king's advisers recommend,

> "Let beautiful young virgins be sought out for the king. And let the king appoint commissioners in all the provinces of his kingdom to gather all the beautiful young virgins to the harem in the citadel of Susa under custody of Hegai, the king's eunuch, who is in charge of the women; let their cosmetic treatments be given them. And let the girl who pleases the king be queen instead of Vashti." This pleased the king, and he did so. (Esther 2:2-4)

John Ortberg's commentary on this section of Esther's story is a kind of tongue-in-cheek critique of contemporary American culture.

> Now we really have to get into this because this was a long time ago, in a really weird world, nothing like the world we live in today. . . . Imagine turning the process of selecting a spouse into a public contest where you bring a group of attractive young women all together and they all vie for the affections of one single bachelor. [Images of the television show *The Bachelor*, based on this exact premise, flash on screen while John continues.]
>
> They all try to see who can please him the most, who can be the most charming, the most pretty. They all get to know each other this process and they find likes and dislikes and rivalries . . . and one by one they drop out until finally one single girl remains. And the bachelor tells her that she's the one that he wants to end up with. What a stupid way to pick a spouse! You have to understand the Bible is lampooning

this process as hopelessly moronic. Aren't you glad we live in a more enlightened age?

Can you believe that there was once a culture where it would be a mark of status for a man that he could land a younger woman of beauty and charm? She would be like a trophy, like a trophy wife?

Can you believe there once was a culture where a man would say, "I have a hot wife" and believe it would be taken seriously as a reason why he should be invited to lead a nation?

In the midst of this narcissistic, sexist, and unjust culture we meet Esther. Humor, both in the book of Esther itself and in its exposition, is used to soften the horrifying realities of oppression. As John Goldingay writes, "The king's beauty contest is pathetic and laughable. But its victims are a series of young teenage girls who have their first (involuntary) sexual experience in the bed of this older man and are then shunted off into his post-coital harem as people with the status of secondary wives but never to be seen again." This is the context our heroine is taken into. The complexity of Esther's background, position, and her lack of recorded words all intensify the drama of the story.

First, Esther is bicultural. She is a Jew named Hadassah living in the capital of the Persian Empire. Raised by her cousin Mordecai, Hadassah is acquainted with Jewish law and custom and simultaneously steeped in Persian language and culture. As Esther is taken into the king's harem, Mordecai instructs her to pass for Persian and not reveal her Jewish heritage. In other words, to be silent about her ethnic and cultural identity. Given the precarious social position of the Jewish people, this must have seemed like a necessary strategy to keep Esther safe. Imagine the vulnerability Esther must have carried, fearing to associate too closely with her Jewish family, culture, or perspective.

My daughter experienced the tensions of being bicultural recently. All the Asian American kids from her class were being grouped together for a "multicultural" event, and my older daughter was grouped with the white kids. As someone who identifies as Filipino American, this was disorienting for her. When she suggested that she might belong with the other group one of her friends said, "Wait, you're Asian?" At that moment our daughter felt invisible, unseen, and frustrated.

I remember thinking, *If this is what "passing" feels like, it's no positive solution to marginalization.* Esther's passing came with profound vulnerability.

Second, Esther found favor.

> The word translated "favor" is the covenant term *hesed* (usually used to describe God's loving kindness and mercy towards his people). Esther wins advantages: she gets beauty treatments, food parcels and maids straightaway. The emphasis is on the speed of obtaining these gifts rather than the fact that these were exceptional presents. . . . Esther is also promoted (lit. "transferred") to *the best place in the harem.*

This process of favor and promotion continues until Esther is made queen. Debra Reid points out, "Esther has assumed Vashti's crown and position, and in doing so, she, like her predecessor, is both honored and at risk."

There's a saying: "Favor ain't fair!" I'd never heard that expression before I started working closely with Caribbean students who were largely from the Pentecostal tradition. Whatever the intended message of that particular slogan, I mostly observed it used to deflect jealousy. It was a quip to deflect unwanted criticism and attention in response to a particular grade, opportunity, or fashion choice. The flip side of Esther's favor is her vulnerability within the social network of the palace. One wrong move, one wrong word, and Esther could find herself exposed, undermined, rejected, or worse.

"Upward mobility can socially isolate people, especially women, in our community," Noemi said as we talked about the resonances of the story of Esther in the Latinx community. "When I was a student in the early 2000s, I remember looking at the psychological impact of higher education on women in my community. At that time, Latina women with a master's degree or higher were much more likely to experience anxiety or depression than women in other communities." "Why do you think that was true?" I asked. "It's because of the isolation women feel," she said. "On the one hand, your family is proud of you for your accomplishment, on the other hand you learn a new language and perspective for your particular profession or field of study. Your family doesn't understand that world or the ways it influences you. You feel estranged at home. At the same time, you are often a minority within the field, so you don't fit there either."

Third, Esther is quiet. Despite being the book's namesake, none of Esther's words are recorded before chapter four. Esther keeps quiet about her people, about the oppressive structure she finds herself within, and in front of the king, only asking for those things she'd been coached to request. This accelerates the plot tension.

Will Esther speak? Will she defy the king? What will this mean for her? These tensions are already bubbling under the surface of the story. Vashti said no, and it cost her the throne. Esther is keeping quiet, but that can't last forever. We understand this as readers. The great Russian playwright Chekhov taught, "If in the first act you have a pistol hanging on the wall, then it must fire in the last act." We've seen the gun. We know, intuitively, if not explicitly, that it's got to go off.

The dramatic tension of the plot continues to mount as Haman, an adviser to the king, creates a scheme to have all the Jews exterminated. Haman concocts this plan out of spite because Mordecai refuses to bow before him, despite the king's command. "When Haman saw that Mordecai did not bow down or do obeisance to him, Haman was infuriated. But he thought it beneath him to lay hands on Mordecai alone. So, having been told who Mordecai's people were, Haman plotted to destroy all the Jews, the people of Mordecai, throughout the whole kingdom of Ahasuerus" (Esther 3:5-6). With the king's permission Haman abuses the legal system to carry out his will, setting a day when every Jewish person in the empire is to be slaughtered. Haman is behaving just like the king. He too shows off his status, wealth, and connection to power and expects absolute obedience. Defiance is met with annihilation.

What will Esther do? Will she risk her life and challenge the king? Will she succeed or fail in her effort to save her people? Will she end up like Vashti or worse?

Esther's first recorded words do not resolve the tension.

> All the king's servants and the people of the king's provinces know that if any man or woman goes to the king inside the inner court without being called, there is but one law—all alike are to be put to death. Only if the king holds out the golden scepter to someone, may that person live. I myself have not been called to come in to the king for thirty days. (Esther 4:11)

Esther is isolated from her community. She's isolated in her role, even as queen. And still, the invitation to her is a risk.

Hesed: God's Favor and Invitation

"There's a strong emotional response to inviting marginalized people to risk," Noemi said. "You're asking us to increase our vulnerability." She's right. Why invite someone like Jonathan, who's already exposed to prejudice, racism, and cultural displacement, to the deeper risks of leadership in these areas? Isn't this just passing along the costs of injustice?

Esther's story fascinates in its complexity. Popular culture celebrates the expressive individualist willing to press against authority and conformity. We lionize our activists, artists, and nonconformists, extolling their courage. When Esther says, "I will go to the king, though it is against the law; and if I perish, I perish" (Esther 4:16), we want to see the expressive individualist hero fighting the system. But is that fair to the story? Esther's next steps demonstrate instead incredible restraint, shrewdness, and agency along with courage.

While God is not mentioned at all in the book of Esther, his character of covenant faithfulness is on every page. Esther's advocacy embodies the covenant faithfulness of God (*hesed*) in the midst of oppression, isolation, and loneliness. Following Esther's story, we can learn to embrace risk in response to the character of God and the complexity of our world.

"Go, gather all the Jews to be found in Susa, and hold a fast on my behalf, and neither eat nor drink for three days, night or day. I and my maids will also fast as you do. After that I will go to the king" (Esther 4:16). Esther's fast connects her deeply to her Jewish roots and to her community. This action situates Esther in the covenant. By fasting, Esther is invoking Deuteronomy 30, where the Lord invites his people to return, even in the midst of exile, and promises God's restorative provision. In a book full of feasts, Esther's fast is a stark and powerful contrast. Esther is still vulnerable, but she embraces risk after anchoring herself in the covenant faithfulness of God.

Speaking of President Obama, Jonathan writes, "*He* was not who we were waiting for and neither are *we*." Rather than get stuck in the lonely spiral of activism, Jonathan has learned to anchor his work in the character of God. He concluded our conversation:

> If my sense of being seen, valued, celebrated, and included comes from my engagement in activism (or slacktivism), I'm not engaged in the work for others but for myself. This isolates me more and more. But, if I'm seen, valued, celebrated, and included because that's who God says I am, it's totally different. I'm free to love others, even as I challenge them.

Jonathan, like Esther, is free to risk because of the character of God.

Esther's restraint is striking throughout. We expect Esther to burst into the king's presence as a supplicant, and having won the king's favor, to depose Haman publicly. Instead, Esther carefully orchestrates her steps. She throws a banquet to honor the king, both playing to his narcissism and positioning him to agree in advance to her request before she's made it. Knowing that the king is impulsive, proud, and deeply concerned about his reputation, Esther sets up the confrontation in private. None of these steps guarantees her success, but they, too, demonstrate the covenant faithfulness of God.

Restraint is not weakness. God has not abandoned his people, even though their need is great. God is at work within the chaotic and corrupted power games of the empire. God has given Esther favor in the form of a royal position and opportunity to go to the king. God's *hesed* has situated Esther for this task. God has blessed

Esther with the wisdom to be able to negotiate complex political realities as a bicultural woman in a position of subjugation. Esther's intentional, restrained, and effective advocacy points beyond itself. It evokes God's character, hidden but not distant, powerful but not domineering.

Broadway composer Sheldon Harnick cut a song from the Broadway musical *Fiddler on the Roof* before its debut in 1964. The song is called "When Messiah Comes." It didn't fit the dramatic arc of the play to introduce a comedic song on the heels of the Jewish community's exile from the village of Anatevka. Nevertheless, the chorus captures this dual sense of God's simultaneous provision and restraint.

> Since that day
> Many men said to us, "Get thee out,"
> Kings they were, gone they are . . .
> We're still here.

This song emerged from longsuffering. Exile and dislocation are etched into the story of God's people. And yet the kings and rulers they were exiled under are long lost to history. "We're still here" is the restrained, humorous, and defiant response.

Esther's story also points to the character of God by demonstrating the reality and complexity of justice. Haman's plot is foiled. The Jewish people are saved. Haman dies on the gallows he'd built to hang Mordecai. And yet complexities remain. Esther remains a "loyal subject and queen" to an oppressive, sexist, and narcissistic ruler. Empowered by the king's support and edict, the Jewish community launches a preemptive attack on those who hated them. These are hard turns for modern readers. We want to see advocacy lead to utopia. We want to see justice restored and ambiguities removed. Esther's story doesn't deliver a utopian vision, but neither does it soft-pedal justice.

The covenant God is just and merciful. Only God can bring both without distortion.

Jonathan's story about "how racism is ruining his marriage" is not, in the end, a tragic story about isolation and hopelessness. His piece concludes,

> The oppressive, corrosive, divisive system of racism and prejudice is as high, long, wide, and deep as anything that I have ever known save for the love of Christ; for the breadth, depth, width and height of the love of God is powerfully boundless and overcomes all hatred and casts out all fear. Yes, racism is destroying me and my marriage but by God's grace we are pressed down but not crushed, persecuted but not abandoned, struck down but not destroyed. Yes, outwardly we are wasting away, but God is renewing us inwardly every day. It is not the cobbled together philosophy of feminism, tolerance or gender and racial equity that holds Priscilla and I together.

Esther's story speaks to us in the vulnerabilities and loneliness in the midst of our work for justice, fairness, and equity. It calls us to embrace risk as women and men anchored in the character of God. Enter the story. Experience the vulnerability, oppression, and exploitation. Observe Esther's courage and restraint, her justice and mercy. Tune your ears and heart to wonder. See how Esther's actions point beyond themselves, reflecting the unnamed and yet very present God of Israel. Now consider your cultural engagement, your activism, and your work for justice. What might God's call to risk mean for you?

For Reflection and Discussion

1. How have you been involved in civil activism in person or online this year? Has this affected your sense of connection to others?

2. What parts of Esther's story resonate with you? What parts

are troubling? How might God be speaking to you through this story?

3. In what ways is God inviting you to risk for the sake of others? How do you feel about that?

4. What would it look like for you to root your activism in God's character?

8 | Ponder

B. J. FOGG, the father of persuasive technology, said, "We can now create machines that can change what people think and what people do, and the machines can do that autonomously." There's a reason why every app on your cell phone signals you to "turn on notifications." There's a reason why every social media site offers the ability to like, love, share, and comment. There's a reason Amazon recommends "people like you also enjoyed . . ." Even as I type these sentences, a buzzing in my pocket signals me that it's time to pick up my phone again. These tools are changing us, accelerating a natural tendency in ways that are unprecedented.

There's some debate about what this technology is doing to reshape how we think. Some researchers claim that the average attention span has declined over the last ten years to nine seconds, from twenty seconds. Curiously, all the research done on attention span is funded by and focused on effective ways to connect a message to our core psychological needs and create behavioral triggers. (It vibrates or pings and we look.) Communications technology is increasingly good at triggering a dopamine response to reinforce compulsive behaviors: buy the kinds of experiences, technology, food, or media that will get

the most likes. Bombarded with efforts to hijack reflection for
the sake of bottom-line consumer growth, is it any wonder
we're more distracted?

Once the cell phone goes dark, the anxiety starts to rise. A few
years ago, we launched a relationships and sexuality course for
college students at a mid-semester conference. Students loved the
sense of safety and trust we'd designed for the track. They engaged
well in Scripture study and small group discussions. Students
raised hard questions about body image, gender identity, recovery
from sexual violence, desire, and holiness. It was going great.

Then we asked students to put their cell phones into a box for
three and a half hours so they would be undistracted as they connected with people in *real life* during free time. You could feel the
anxiety level in the room shoot up. Several students laughed un-
comfortably, assuming that we were joking. Some students started
bargaining, "But I was going to use my phone to study" or, my
favorite, "My Bible is on my phone, and I'd really hoped to read it."
I was fascinated. We'd been talking about serious topics and
sharing deeply and honestly. How could it be easier for college
students to talk vulnerably about sex than be without their
cell phones?

"How did you feel without your phone?" Carolyn asked as students came back together. "I felt naked," one student said. Others
described instinctively reaching for their pocket and feeling a
tinge of panic when they realized their phone wasn't there.
Carolyn continued, "How did being without your phone impact
how you spent time?" The room got quiet. "I was really mad at
first," Stephen said, "but then I figured there's nothing I can do
about it now. I decided to go outside and play ultimate Frisbee
with students from our campus." Carolyn leaned in, "If you'd had
your phone, would you have played?" Stephen thought for a
second, "Probably not," he said.

Today's Cigarettes

As a former smoker I recognized the experience students were describing. I had my first cigarette at the age when many kids get their own smartphone. By high school I was smoking a pack of twenty cigarettes, or more, a day. I kept a fan in my room, blowing out year-round, so that the first thing I could do in the morning was have a cigarette. I smoked before I went to bed too. Smoking cigarettes gave me something to do with the awkward feelings I often had in social situations. It also created a connection with other smokers, giving someone a light or a cigarette is an unspoken custom among smokers and easily leads to small talk. By the time I arrived at college I was thoroughly hooked. In those days, if you'd taken my cigarettes away, I'd have felt vulnerable, angry, and disoriented. I'd have laughed or groaned in disbelief if you'd asked me to put my cigarettes in a box for a few hours in order to interact with people. I'd have said, and believed, "If you want me to interact with people, the last thing you want to do is take the cigarettes away. Trust me."

A short time after this conference I heard smartphones described as "today's cigarettes." Heavily marketed toward children as a symbol of maturity and adulthood while simultaneously highly addictive, smartphones occupy the place in our culture once held by Philip Morris and R. J. Reynolds. We know that smoking causes serious health problems, including cancer, emphysema, and heart disease. We don't know the long-term health implications of smartphones, but anxiety, depression, and loneliness have skyrocketed in parallel with the adoption of these technologies. Are we addicted? Have we adapted our behavior, as the designers have hoped, so that we escape into our devices every time we feel awkward, bored, lonely, or a notification signals to us that we're missing out? Is it possible that these habits are actually distancing us from the relationships and connections we need to thrive?

Some people find deep and meaningful relational connections among the churn of contemporary communication technologies. Many find it isolating. Every hour invested in YouTube videos is an hour not spent on relationships in real life. Distraction, in our contemporary age, is leveraged and accelerated with an aim to transform our behavior, mostly to get us to buy stuff. From a purely persuasive design standpoint, our social disequilibrium is a positive outcome if it can be converted into product sales.

God did not design us for distraction and social disorientation but for life and relationship. Our natural inclination toward distraction is not a barrier to life with God or to life in relationship with others but a context in which we can discover tools to enrich both.

Three times in the Gospel of Luke, Mary, the mother of Jesus, is said to "ponder." Pondering changes Mary's perspective, enabling her to participate in God's saving work, even at great risk. Pondering increases Mary's compassion, reflecting the character of God. Pondering opens Mary to new possibilities about what God is doing in Jesus and what that might mean for her. God, through the story of Mary, invites us to ponder. As we hear and respond to God's invitation, we will discover how pondering leads us to be present to others in ways that deepen our relational connections and lift our sense of loneliness.

Mary: Pondering and Waiting

"It isn't fair," Melina said. "How come Zechariah asks the angel a question and is struck dumb, but Mary asks the angel the same question and it's okay?" Other students resonated with Melina's question. This was our second Bible study in the Gospel of Luke, and I was grateful for the energy such a direct challenge created.

Luke opens his Gospel with two angelic birth announcements. Each deeply resonates with the story of Israel. Zechariah's announcement happens in the temple. Echoes of Isaiah 6, where God calls Isaiah in the temple, as well as stories of childless couples whose long-awaited son carries God's story forward (see Abraham and Sarah in Genesis 21, Rachel and Jacob in Genesis 30 and 35, the birth of Samson in Judges 13, and Samuel in 1 Samuel 1) are intentionally sounded throughout the section. Here the angel Gabriel announces that Zechariah and his wife will have a son who will prepare the way for the Lord's coming. Such a son is an answer to the prayers not simply of a childless couple getting on in years but of the whole people of God who have been praying for Israel's redemption. The whole point of restored temple worship, of keeping Torah, of praying for the redemption of Israel was, according to this angelic messenger, moving forward with the birth of John. Zechariah should have been beside himself with joy, but he's suspicious. Despite Zechariah's lineage and training as a priest and his "blamelessness" under the law, Zechariah's response is disbelief. "Zechariah said to the angel, 'How will I know that this is so? For I am an old man, and my wife is getting on in years'" (Luke 1:18).

As a result of Zechariah's disbelief, the angel Gabriel says, "Because you did not believe my words, which will be fulfilled in their time, you will become mute, unable to speak, until the day these things occur" (v. 20). Zechariah's request for a sign, "How will I know that this is so?" is answered, though in a way we can easily imagine is different from what Zechariah might have imagined.

Mary's announcement, in contrast, happens outside Jerusalem in the town of Nazareth, in Galilee. Mary does not have Zechariah's lineage or education. She is young, "betrothed in marriage" to Joseph but still living at home. She is in that liminal space between commitment and consummation, on the cusp of adulthood as defined by her culture.

Mary's response to the announcement that she is to conceive and will bear a son who will sit on the throne of David forever is to ask, "How can this be, since I am a virgin?" (v. 34). The angel gives Mary no rebuke for her question but instead shares a poetic explanation that emphasizes the power of God, "overshadowing" Mary and bringing about Jesus' totally unique life.

Mary is not unaware of the risks and vulnerabilities that come with the angelic announcement. Unlike Zechariah, whose wife's pregnancy is a welcome blessing, Mary's pregnancy exposes her to suspicions of adultery, which could lead to her public disgrace, stoning, or quiet dismissal. Despite these great personal risks, Mary's response to the angel is, "Here am I, the servant of the Lord; let it be with me according to your word" (v. 38).

At this point in the story it's important for Protestants to slow down enough to notice what's happening. Mary is unique in the biblical narrative. She is a young woman of no particular pedigree who happens to find "favor with God." When visited by an angel and told that she is to bring Israel's story forward through bearing a son at the wrong time, exposing her to personal risk, she gives an unqualified yes. Abraham prayed that his son Ishmael would inherit the promise, disbelieving that his wife Sarah would bear a son in her old age. Moses complained that he didn't know how to speak and asked God to send someone else. Isaiah cried, "Woe is me." Jacob wrestled. Gideon did that thing with the fleece. But Mary? She simply says yes.

If we read this narrative typologically, it gets even more interesting. Eve, seeing that "the tree was good for food, and that it was a delight to the eyes, and that the tree was to be desired to make one wise, she took of its fruit" (Genesis 3:6). Eve's disobedience was anchored in distrust of God's word, desire for wisdom, longing for the aesthetic pleasure of the forbidden fruit, and grasping after authority. Mary, by contrast, trusts God's word even though the risks of her obedience are significant. Read across the story of Israel, Mary's obedience to God's call is precisely the response of faithfulness and trust that the prophets lament is missing in Israel.

How is it that Mary is able to offer unqualified, trusting obedience to God when prophets, patriarchs, and kings did not? What was it about Mary that enabled her to find favor with God and then respond to God's favor with humble trust? My Roman Catholic friends have answers to these questions, which, I confess, continue to puzzle me as an Anglican. Still, I lament the ways we in the Protestant tradition have tended to be so afraid of exalting or deifying Mary that we're unwilling to see how unique Mary truly is. As a father of daughters, I want my girls to encounter the Mary whose act of courageous obedience puts the prophets and patriarchs to shame. I want my teenage daughters to discover that they are not too young to live a big life with God. I want them to see the pivotal role of women in moving the story of redemption forward.

Mary's response to the angel emerges, at least in part, as the result of pondering. Where Zechariah was overcome by fear, Mary "was much perplexed by his words and pondered what sort of greeting this might be" (Luke 1:29). The verb translated "ponder" in this section is *dialogizomai* (it's related to our word *dialogue*). It means to reason about something thoroughly, to think or argue it out. Despite the pious imagination behind religious art and contemporary cinema, Mary doesn't stare doe-eyed into the middle distance with placid contemplation. She thinks carefully about this strange greeting and what it means for her. This gives her perspective that must have contributed to her obedience.

A few years ago my younger daughter pointed out how pondering in the sense above enabled a different Mary to offer Jesus a unique gift.

ME	Mary [of Bethany] anoints Jesus' feet and wipes them with her hair. This moment is intimate to the point of discomfort. Women did not "let down their hair" in public. To massage Jesus' feet in this way, publicly, is to open herself to disgrace. Why would she do that?
DAUGHTER	Maybe because she listened to Jesus' words and understood that he was going to die soon.
ME	How is it that *she* understood when so many did not?
DAUGHTER	Maybe she paid attention to his words. He did say that he was going to die. And maybe she really thought them through.
ME	*(stunned silence)* So Mary understood Jesus better than his disciples because she took the time to think through [ponder] his words.
DAUGHTER	I think so.
ME	How can we be more like Mary?
DAUGHTER	We can think through what Jesus says.

Mary's risky devotion is rooted in an understanding of what is about to happen to Jesus, which she could only have arrived at through pondering Jesus' words in a way his disciples did not.

It's speculative, but not overly so, to imagine Mary (the mother of Jesus) puzzling out the angelic greeting. If she had, she would have recognized the echoes of Gideon, Moses, and others. Mary would have foreseen the angelic greeting as a precursor of a call to move God's story forward. She would recognize the hand of

God and the long-awaited promise. Thinking it through would give Mary perspective to say yes.

"Oh, I guess Mary's response is pretty different than Zechariah's," Melina said.

Compassion

The image of the Nativity in the popular imagination is indebted to St. Francis. His first effort, celebrated in a cave in Greccio, Italy, on Christmas Eve 1223 included a live donkey and ox. (These animals are not mentioned in the Gospels but seem to have been inferred by European imagination.) Francis's involvement of the local community, his deep affection for Jesus, and his example to his friars made a powerful impact. Eight hundred years later, Francis's creative experiment in worship still sets the imaginative palette for Christian worship at Christmas.

Francis's preaching and perspective not only shape our image of the Nativity but also our interpretive lenses. Mary and Joseph are turned out in the cold by an inn at Bethlehem. They were poor and vulnerable. Poor Mary is forced to deliver in a stable, among livestock, with no one to help. Angels visit the poor, marginal, undeserving shepherds to tell them of Messiah's birth. This picture is deeply resonant with the values and vision of St. Francis, whose embrace of "sister poverty" was central to his ministry. (Francis's spiritual descendants would get into serious conflict over whether having shoes put them on the primrose path to greed and worldliness.)

The Gospels are far less "Franciscan" than we think.

Tradition has them knocking at an inn door, being told there was no room, and then being offered the stable along with the animals. But the word for "inn" in the traditional translations has several meanings, and it's likely that they were, in fact, on the ground floor of a house where people normally stayed upstairs. The ground floor would often be used for animals—hence the manger or feeding-trough, which came in handy for the baby—but there is nothing to say that there were actually animals there at the time.

Similarly, the Gospels never quite seem to adopt the shepherd-as-outcast motif that was present in Aristotle and other ancient writers. (Luke is capable of invoking God's kingdom coming in Jesus for marginal communities, but he doesn't seem to include shepherds in that scheme.)

Right in the middle of this Nativity scene we find Mary pondering a second time. Angels appear to a group of shepherds in Bethlehem and announce that the Messiah has been born in David's city. The shepherds go to Bethlehem to see this child. The manger identifies Mary's son as the promised shepherd king to come. The shepherds are amazed at all that the angels have told them. Those who hear the shepherds' tale are similarly amazed, but Mary ponders.

Luke uses a different Greek term translated "ponder" in this section. This word is more reflective than *dialogizomai*, used in Luke 1:29. Mary's response to the energy and amazement of the shepherds is to reflect. She reflects on the implications of the shepherds' words, transforming amazement into something deeper.

Spiritual writer Ronald Rolheiser writes, "Compassion begins with what the gospels call 'pondering.' To ponder, in the biblical sense, is to resist having energy simply flow through you and instead hold, carry, and transform it so as to not give it back in kind." It's the opposite of the nonreflective, distracted responses we are increasingly conditioned to generate. How easy it would have been for Mary to be caught up in the energy of the shepherds' tale only to have that amazement diffuse once the moment passed.

Pondering transforms the energy, excitement, heat, anger, or fear of our environment. The simple act of "holding" these words enables Mary to be present to the shepherds, to her son, and to the mystery of God's work through her circumstances. Compassion in its truest form is not reactive empathy but thoughtful and willful engagement to alleviate suffering. Mary's pondering prepares her heart for compassion.

What might Mary's pondering and Luke's inclusion of it in the narrative enable us to see? How might it increase our capacity for compassion?

Pondering like Mary, we might be reminded of David, the shepherd boy of Bethlehem. David's life was not romantic, serene, and easy. David was anointed king by Samuel in the middle of Saul's reign. Jesus, David's long-awaited heir, is entering the world as king, even heralded by angels, during the reign of Caesar and Herod. David's anointing led to years of struggle, of being hunted by Saul and rejected by his people. What might this mean for the baby sleeping in the manger?

We might be reminded that the Messiah is called to be the true shepherd of God's people, the one who will care for the vulnerable, search for the lost, provide for the hungry. Who better to receive this announcement than the shepherds of Bethlehem? Pondering the shepherds' words might remind Mary that her sleeping infant will be intimately acquainted with the vulnerable, lost, hungry, and harassed. What will this mean for her family?

When our girls were small, we worshiped alongside women and men wrestling with various types of housing and food instability. Worship ended with a community meal where relationships could form. This led to difficult questions. "Why do people sleep at church? How come people don't have homes to live in?" It also led to perspective. We love and pray for women and men whose lives are marked by homelessness, vulnerability, and other challenges. We look at our housing, warm relationships, and good food as a gift. (For years our girls would pray every night, "God, thank you for a nice, warm bed to sleep in and a safe place to live.")

We don't know how engagement with and care for the poor and hungry were fleshed out in Jesus' early life. We do know it shaped his public ministry. It'd be surprising if his family life hadn't been shaped by Mary's pondering and the ways it led to compassion.

Francis's vision of the Nativity points to compassion. This is part of the reason it's still so powerful. Our distracted, addicted, and desperate age cries out for compassion. Increased visibility of the desperate needs around the corner and around the world signal a need for compassion. Relationship building across difference requires compassion. Mary's pondering presses us to grow in compassion.

Mary's pondering also leads us to a deeper understanding of the work of God in the person of Jesus. Mary had pondered the angelic greeting. She understood who her son was to be, but what a way for God to fulfill his purposes! If God's method for demonstrating his covenant faithfulness comes in the form of shepherds' visits, stories of angels' songs, and the call to serve the vulnerable, what does it say about the character of God? Ponder with Mary the mixture of vulnerability and authority wrapped in swaddling clothes. How might this anchor your compassion? Feel the excitement, weight, and risk before you. Then ask, How do I need to grow in compassion so I might reflect the character of Jesus?

Possibilities

The third time Mary ponders in Luke 2 is when Jesus is twelve years old.

Every year his parents went to Jerusalem for the festival of the Passover. And when he was twelve years old, they went up as usual for the festival. When the festival was ended and they started to return, the boy Jesus stayed behind in Jerusalem, but his parents did not know it. Assuming that he was in the group of travelers, they went a day's journey. Then they started to look for him among their relatives and friends. When they did not find him, they returned to Jerusalem to search for him. After three days they found him in the temple, sitting among the teachers, listening to them and asking them questions. And all who heard him were amazed at his understanding and his answers. When his parents saw him they were astonished; and his mother said to him, "Child, why have you treated us like this? Look, your father and I have been searching for you in great anxiety." He said to them, "Why were you searching for me? Did you not know that I must be in my Father's house?" But they did not understand what he said to them. Then he went down with them and came to Nazareth, and was obedient to them. His mother treasured all these things in her heart. (Luke 2:41-51)

This passage is a masterful part of Luke's storytelling. Jesus on the cusp of manhood goes to Jerusalem. His journey to Jerusalem dominates the second half of Luke's Gospel. Discovering that Jesus is not on their return trip, Mary and Joseph rush back to Jerusalem and search for Jesus for three days. Luke's Gospel ends with two disciples rushing back to Jerusalem after "finding" the resurrected Jesus in their company, after three days. Jesus' words correct Mary's perspective. Luke's Gospel ends with Jesus correcting the two disciples on the road to Emmaus, "Oh, how foolish you are, and how slow of heart to believe all that the prophets have declared!" (Luke 24:25).

Mary's treasuring Jesus' words signals a change in expectations. Jesus' vocation is not going to meet Mary's expectations
but will reframe them. Everyone expected the Messiah to cleanse
the temple. Jesus' zeal for his father's house will result in his
being rejected, arrested, and crucified. No one expected that.
Luke is not sentimentalizing Mary, as though "treasuring these
things in her heart" meant capturing a moment for the family
memories album. He's signaling that something significant is
happening in this story and begging us to treasure its significance with her.

If we ponder this story, what might we see? We'll see Mary's
concern over losing her son, and we'll recognize that this loss is a
mere foretaste of what's to come. We might see that Jesus' vocation
is somehow inextricably linked to the temple, to Jerusalem, and
to the Passover. We notice Jesus reframing expectations of what
his messiahship might mean. We'll notice that Mary, as before, is
willing to ponder these strange movements and transform them
as well as be transformed by them.

⬤

I threw my dish into the sink so hard I was surprised it didn't
break. I was fuming. I'd promised God I'd apply for InterVarsity
Christian Fellowship staff and to Shakespeare & Company, and
that whichever one he wanted me to do he'd open up. That week
I'd received an invitation to both. It was heart wrenching. On one
hand, I wanted to pursue God's call to missions and ministry. On
the other hand, there was no good reason I could see to not continue my career as an actor/artist. Though I didn't know it at the
time, I'd blamed God for my acting work drying up in 1995 and
the disappointments and fears that came as a result. My inner
logic was simple: *Okay, God, if you're calling me to something*

else . . . Fine! This monologue was blissfully unaware of the fact that it came through clenched teeth. Ah, but now, now I had an opportunity to work at one of the premier Shakespeare theaters in the country. Why tease me with a golden opportunity and muddle my deeply spiritual—if I do say so myself—commitment to follow God's call?

"Jason, look up!" I heard a voice say. I looked around the room. I was alone. Never before had I heard an audible voice I believed to be the voice of God. "Look up!" The voice said again. Lifting my head and gazing out my apartment window I was suddenly overwhelmed by the beauty of that early spring day. Tiny tufts of green were poking out of the brown earth. The trees shimmered with a hint of new foliage. The last remnants of snow were finally melted. It took my breath away.

"I created all of this beauty from nothing," the voice continued. "I made you. Why don't you trust that I can make something beautiful out of your life? I will not make your decisions for you."

I've never had an experience like that again, but it is an experience I treasure. At that moment Jesus reshaped my expectations about life and ministry, opening me to possibilities I'd never fully considered. Twenty years later I'm so grateful for this call and intervention (no clenched teeth).

Jesus still transforms lives and expectations. He is at work reconfiguring our hearts, increasing our compassion, giving us perspective as participants in his kingdom agenda. We can participate in this work when we, like Mary, ponder.

Desert father Abba Poemen described the impact of pondering this way. "The nature of water is soft, that of stone is hard; but if a bottle is hung above the stone, allowing the water to fall drop by drop, it wears away the stone. So it is with the word of God; it is soft, and our heart is hard, but the one who hears the word of God often, opens his heart to the fear of God."

To ponder like Mary means making time to reflect carefully and think through implications. It means holding the excitements, anxieties, and outrage of our moment long enough to transform them in the presence of God. Pondering means orchestrating space by putting devices away and attending to the discomfort and addictions that drive us. Pondering means being open to God doing a new thing in our lives, community, or sense of call.

As we ponder, we create more space for developing relationships. As I reflected on the story of Mary, I began to notice how many relationships in the midst of a busy ministry and home life were completely reflexive. We talk without thinking, listen without hearing, comment without considering, and wonder why we're washing the dishes of a lively gathering while our guts ache with a sense of isolation. The same thing can be said about life with God. We chatter on in prayer, rehearsing our anxieties, wants, or wishes, apologizing for not measuring up to our own hopes and expectations, and rush off to the next thing without really considering how we might live more present to God in the coming moments.

For Reflection and Discussion

1. How would you describe distraction in your life? What contributes to it? How is it affecting your relationships?

2. What stood out to you about Mary's character in this chapter? What puzzles you?

3. How might God be inviting you to ponder? What structures might be necessary to help you respond to God's invitation?

4. How might you design times and spaces for pondering, compassion, and relationship building in real life?

9 | Follow

HERE we go," Tim said as we pressed the heavy door to the bishop's office. Tim Strabbing and I served together as the wardens of our parish church. Earlier that day the bishop's office had called summoning us to a meeting. The sky was overcast, gray and brown like the stones of the cathedral, making the large oak door the brightest and warmest spot on the grounds. Crossing the threshold feels like stepping back through time into a castle or Edwardian estate renovated sometime in the 1990s. The reception area is a brightly lit hallway with large portraits on one side and antique books on the other.

Bishop Andy is a pink-faced man with a white beard and bright eyes. His shape, gait, and crinkle around his eyes when smiling have rightly earned him the nickname Santa Claus, though I always think of him as Papa Smurf. He ushered us into his office warmly and seated us in a small reception area away from his desk.

"I'll get straight to the point," he said, still warmly but with a slight constriction in his gut making his voice a little thinner. "I've removed your pastor from his duties effective immediately." I'd been expecting something difficult ever since I got the phone call summoning us to an urgent meeting with the bishop. It was a Tuesday afternoon in the middle of December, hardly a slow time of year for the church. Still the weight of his words seemed to take most of the air out of the room. He continued, "According to the laws and governance of our church, this means you are in charge." All the air was gone now.

The bishop kept talking, explaining the church's disciplinary process, his reasons for the decision, and the logistical decisions we needed to make in order to cooperate with his office. "Of course, you'll need to announce this decision to your congregation this weekend," I heard the bishop's voice say.

The coming weekend was our annual Christmas pageant. Kids dressed as oxen and sheep would be crawling around the sanctuary. Miniature shepherds would try to corral these distracted toddlers while angels sang and wise men processed with their golden parcels. While some church pageants are examples of harmonious intergenerational collaboration—sparking oohs and ahs from visiting families, drawing visitors from near and far, and astonishing all with musical talent—our pageant is more like a karaoke party on roller skates hosted by an elementary school. It's impressive, in its own way, and totally chaotic. (I've come to appreciate the pageant all the more for this quality, but this may be a quirk.) How were we going to stand in front of the congregation in the afterglow and chaos of this worship service and tell our congregation that a beloved pastor, one who may have performed their wedding, baptized their children, and visited them in the hospital, was gone and not coming back? There would surely be speculation, strong emotion, and perhaps even hostility. There would be good questions I couldn't answer. Even sitting beside two partners in ministry, Tim and Christine, I felt the weight of responsibility, anxiety, and isolation.

Two days later Sophia took me to lunch. She looked at me with sympathetic scrutiny. "I need you to look at me and tell me clearly that you sense Jesus calling you to lead our church over this next season," she said. "You already have a demanding full-time ministry. Leading through this kind of transition is going to be costly." Sophia leaned in closely. "If Jesus is calling you to lead, then I will support and bless you wholeheartedly, but if you can't look me in the eyes and tell me this is an invitation from God, then I don't think you should do it, and you won't have my blessing."

These kinds of conversations were not what I'd envisioned when Sophia and I covenanted to a life in ministry together. We'd envisioned our home full of friends, building communities on campus, and investing together in projects and programs alongside the poor. We'd envisioned late-night discipleship conversations. We envisioned a beautiful simplicity in life leading to a deep sense of stability. We never imagined the daily demands of organizational leadership filling our days with complexity while simultaneously leading a church community through crisis. Leading the church through betrayal, confusion, denial, anger, and loss would mean less space to process our own feelings. It would mean late nights, weighty decisions, and the inability to talk to others about the complexity. Somehow when we imagined ministry together, we never imagined feeling stretched, isolated, and lonely.

Loneliness and Ministry

Loneliness, betrayal, and disappointment are often surprising to the young campus ministers I've hired, inducted, trained, coached, and supervised through the years. They will light up with emotion discussing their call to campus mission, how they've discerned God's call, and how excited they are to begin work. New York City Area Ministry Director Tim Craig recently wrote about his experience this way.

After applying for a campus ministry role and interviewing, I took a morning, prayed, fasted, and spent time in

Luke 5:1-11, the same passage where I first sensed a call to ministry.

As I met with Jesus that morning, a couple things became very clear. First, Jesus was on my boat. He would be with me wherever I went and whatever decision was made. Secondly, his presence with me calmed the fear in my soul and clarified the calling to New York City. Just as I had felt afraid when first called to ministry, so again his words spoke peace to my soul: "Don't be afraid; from now on you will fish for people."

What a great picture of reassurance. Tim didn't need to be afraid of the call to ministry because Jesus was with him, calling him to fish for people like Peter, James, and John. Tim then moved from Rochester to New York City.

Newly married, with no contacts in New York, Tim moved into a neighborhood where he is an ethnic minority, a new experience for him, and jumped in to ministry at two elite conservatories. His early years were excruciating. The cultural-adjustment curve for Tim as he negotiated starting life in a new neighborhood and city was much more difficult than he imagined. Students rejected Tim's efforts to support them in ministry. Campus administrations were suspicious of Tim's presence. After a year of hard work and partnership, a campus ministry partner realigned ministry that they had been doing together with her local church, functionally excluding Tim from a mission he'd helped to build.

I remember walking with Tim at our annual leadership conference. After three years of not being able to bring a single student to this conference, Tim had succeeded in bringing two students. Now, two days into the conference, unhappy with our campus mission and blaming Tim, these students were leaving. If I were Tim I might have felt set up. "Okay, God, I'm following you to New York City because that's how I understood your call, but I'm frustrated. Did you call me here to make a fool of me?"

Paul: A Lonely Calling

Following God's call into mission can be lonely. Crises of faith emerge when, after hearing God's call and stepping into God's mission, ministers experience betrayal, rejection, and disappointment. What do you do when your motives, character, and connections are questioned? The apostle Paul knew about loneliness in mission. From his call on the road to Damascus to his pastoral epistles, we see a man who is simultaneously gripped by the beauty and wonder of the gospel and deeply acquainted with isolation, loneliness, challenge, and heartbreak. We can learn a great deal by considering Paul's call to follow Jesus despite loneliness and challenge. In Paul's story we discover the beauty of God's grace, a sustaining vision greater than loneliness or rejection.

The hints of Paul's missionary challenges are anchored in his conversion.

> Meanwhile Saul, still breathing threats and murder against the disciples of the Lord, went to the high priest and asked him for letters to the synagogues at Damascus, so that if he found any who belonged to the Way, men or women, he might bring them bound to Jerusalem. Now as he was going along and approaching Damascus, suddenly a light from heaven flashed around him. He fell to the ground and heard a voice saying to him, "Saul, Saul, why do you persecute me?" He asked, "Who are you, Lord?" The reply came, "I am Jesus, whom you are persecuting. But get up and enter the city, and you will be told what you are to do." The men who were traveling with him stood speechless because they heard the voice but saw no one. Saul got up from the ground,

and though his eyes were open, he could see nothing; so they led him by the hand and brought him into Damascus. For three days he was without sight, and neither ate nor drank. (Acts 9:1-9)

Paul was sending himself on missionary projects of a sort before he knew Jesus. His zeal for God led him to displace himself in order to bring this movement of Jesus followers down. His life as a persecutor of the church literally embodies the opposition he would later experience as an apostle and missionary. Armed with arrest warrants he sets out for Damascus with fellow collaborators, and he has a life-changing encounter with the risen Jesus.

This experience changes everything Paul understands about himself and about what it means to worship God. Before his confrontation with Jesus, Paul would have understood himself as a teacher of Israel, as light to the Gentiles, and as one who saw clearly into the law of God. Paul would have seen himself as fighting on God's behalf against those who'd threaten the Jewish way of life. Through a flash of light and a powerful voice, Paul now understands that he's been fighting against God and against his Messiah. In something of an enacted parable, the one who thought he could see fumbles around in the darkness, blinded by his first encounter with real light.

Imagine what it must have been like for Paul to be so radically reoriented as he sat in the darkness of those three days. Paul is not who he thinks he is. Not only are his allegiances wrong but he's doing the very thing he wants desperately to avoid. By attacking the church, Paul is pushing against the purposes of God, not protecting them. Paul's scholarship, his religious training, his connections in the temple and among the Pharisees are all being upended. Paul's physical blindness points to his spiritual blindness. It opens him to considering possibilities he'd never imagined.

After the initial wave of disappointment began to settle at church, we started looking carefully at our life and ministry. Why didn't we know the extent to which our pastor's life and ministry were unraveling? What signs and symptoms of his impending crisis should we have caught? How, as a leader, had I failed to intervene when I should have?

We started noticing areas of deep organizational dysfunction. Fear of conflict crippled our ability to work through hard issues. Without the ability to have healthy conflict, things that should have raised an alarm were held in confidence. Trust that sensitive issues could be raised in a healthy way and dealt with appropriately eroded. Accountability was inconsistent at best.

Looking more closely at my own leadership was painful and disorienting. I'd thought I was helping this pastor to succeed, but was this true? Over my tenure in leadership at the church, I'd seen our pastor become increasingly disengaged in ministry but didn't confront this trend nearly as robustly as I should have. I watched him make what I thought were bad decisions and failed to challenge them. Most pointedly, I'd believed it was past time for this pastor to transition out of his role, perhaps out of pastoral ministry for a season, but rather than act on this and press toward a resolution, I chose to support him, hoping that he'd come to the conclusion to leave on his own. In each of these ways I believed I was helping but instead was adding to the dysfunction in the system. Wanting desperately to help our church to become healthy, I had been making it worse.

I felt like there was a twenty-pound bowling ball hung around my neck and another one in an invisible backpack. When people write about leadership being lonely, I think they are trying to capture this sensation. The weight of responsibility presses down and refuses to let up. Friends, colleagues, and coworkers may offer support, encouragement, even partnership, but it doesn't take away the sensation of dead weight that comes with responsibility.

Sitting in the dark with Paul was illuminating. Like Paul, I'd been blind to the truth, leading with great energy in ways that were costly to God's people. Like Paul, I was humbled. Like Paul, I needed to see myself differently.

●

Can you imagine what it was like for him? Paul, the great agitator and leader, needed to be led by the hand into the city. How humbling—if not humiliating—this must have been. Zealous to do the work of God, Paul had been kicking against the God of Israel and his Messiah, Jesus. Paul's basic understanding of who God is turned out not just to be wrong but wrong in ways that cost Stephen his life and others their freedom. Paul, the activist whose keen mind and strong will put him on the road to Damascus, sat in the dark for three days, waiting to be told—by one of the "heretics" he'd come to round up—what he needed to do.

Sitting in the dark for three days seems terribly inefficient, especially to those of us who live in the twenty-first century, which Thomas Friedman describes as "an age of accelerations" in his book *Thank You for Being Late*.

Blind Days

Paul stays blind over these seventy-two hours, fasting, praying, and pondering with no guarantees about what's next. These days seem inefficient to us, in part because we radically underestimate the amount of time it takes to process and integrate new information, especially when that information challenges our sense of identity, accomplishment, competence, or relationships. As disorienting and lonely as it must have been for Paul, time was just what he needed.

In these blind days God was forming a new identity for Paul, one based entirely on the grace, generosity, and beauty of Christ. The beauty of God's grace in Jesus comes in the details of Jesus' confrontation with Paul on the road to Damascus. Paul was comfortable dealing out prison and death to those who opposed his vision of what it meant to be the people of God. But Jesus' response to being persecuted by Paul isn't to get a warrant for his arrest or even to stand by approvingly while Paul is stoned to death as a heretic, but to provide Paul with an opportunity to know him. Discovering that he was persecuting the Messiah, Paul would have approved of his own death sentence. But Jesus is not interested in the death of the wicked but in costly, self-giving restoration and relationship. This love is confrontational, perhaps even combative, but it is unrelentingly merciful.

In these blind days God shows Paul a vision of a man named Ananias coming and laying hands on him in the name of Jesus that his sight might be restored. This is more than Paul might have dared to hope. Moses failed to honor God's holiness in front of the people at the waters of Meribah, and as a result he was not able to lead the people into the Promised Land (Numbers 20:2-13). Paul was literally persecuting the people of God, but his sin is forgiven, his sight is restored, and he is included in the family of Jesus.

In these blind days God also shows Paul that he is to be a messenger of Jesus before Gentiles, kings, and the people of Israel. As a Pharisee and religious teacher, Paul believed that his vocation was to renew covenant faithfulness in Israel so God's blessing would come to Israel and finally would pass through Israel to the world. The zeal of his persecution of the church was in part because he believed a false messiah was a threat to this covenant faithfulness scheme. (If "the Way," as it was called, was exalting Jesus as Messiah and they were wrong, they'd be leading Israel away from covenant faithfulness, directly opposing his understanding of his vocation.) Now, in spite of Paul's violent persecution of the church and his failure to be the light and hope he'd worked so hard to be, Paul is brought into the center of God's mission. This is vocational restoration, by sheer grace making Paul what he longed to be in his zeal and effort but could never accomplish.

Sitting in the dark with Paul contemplating the overwhelming grace of God sustained and reoriented me during this difficult season of leadership at church. As questions and critical feedback started coming in, I would reflect on Paul, on the grace and generosity of God. Instead of nursing resentment, self-pity, or beating myself up for my leadership mistakes, I tried to cultivate wonder at the grace of God for me and for our little church. Paul's prayer in Ephesians 1 became a daily discipline, a chance to anchor myself in and celebrate the riches of God's grace. When bad news or difficult situations came up, and they did, I conditioned myself to say "God is generous" before anything else as a reminder of the wonder of God's grace. There were still hard decisions, disappointments, late nights, and strongly worded emails, but the beauty of God's grace was emotional fuel, propelling us through the difficult times.

Immediately following his conversion and baptism Paul begins to proclaim Jesus. And almost as quickly Paul experiences opposition, challenge, and life-threatening difficulties. The first threat to Paul's life comes within four verses of the record of his conversion, Paul escapes capture and death by being smuggled out of the city in a basket. Escaping with his life, Paul then comes to Jerusalem and tries to join the disciples, but they are all afraid of him, and it takes some advocacy and hard work for relationships to be formed.

This pattern of Paul's ministry continues through the rest of the book of Acts and, from what we know, the rest of his life. Paul engages in powerful preaching and signs of God's power. There is opposition, threats, sometimes even violence. And then Paul experiences challenges and difficulties among the believers. Here are just a few examples of the conflicts, disappointments, and betrayals Paul experienced within the church: Paul's ally and advocate Barnabas parts ways with him after a conflict (Acts 15:36-41); Paul argues publicly with Peter about circumcision and food laws (Galatians 2:11-14); a powerful teacher named Apollos (not coincidentally named for the Greek god of poetry and rhetoric) preaches in the places where Paul had planted churches, causing some to compare Paul and Apollos stylistically and find Paul wanting (1 Corinthians 2:1–3:7).

Paul would experience far worse. Paul endured rejection, even stoning, by fellow Jews (Acts 14:19-20), and flogging and imprisonment from fellow Romans (Acts 16:19-24). In one of his letters to the Corinthians Paul summarized his missionary experience in Asia this way: "We do not want you to be unaware, brothers and sisters, of the affliction we experienced in Asia; for we were so utterly, unbearably crushed that we despaired of life itself. Indeed, we felt that we had received the sentence of death so that we would rely not on ourselves but on God who raises the dead" (2 Corinthians 1:8-9).

For those of us raised on hero stories in which obstacles are overcome, order restored, and "happily ever after" ensues, Paul's story is a useful counterbalance. Sometimes we infer that because Paul was an apostle and author of much of the New Testament, his life and ministry fit the hero-story arc. It doesn't. Paul's pattern of missionary engagement and the ups and downs, betrayals and loneliness, powerful signs and persecution follow Paul all the way to the end of his journey. In one of Paul's last letters he writes,

> Do your best to come to me soon, for Demas, in love with this present world, has deserted me and gone to Thessalonica; Crescens has gone to Galatia, Titus to Dalmatia. Only Luke is with me. Get Mark and bring him with you, for he is useful in my ministry. I have sent Tychicus to Ephesus. When you come, bring the cloak that I left with Carpus at Troas, also the books, and above all the parchments. Alexander the coppersmith did me great harm; the Lord will pay him back for his deeds. You also must beware of him, for he strongly opposed our message. (2 Timothy 4:9-15)

During these long seasons of challenge, Paul was sustained by his call to follow Jesus as an apostle and witness. This invitation is embedded in Paul's conversion and is threaded throughout his missionary life. Speaking about Paul to Ananias while Paul is waiting in the dark, God says, "he is an instrument whom I have chosen to bring my name before Gentiles and kings and before the people of Israel; I myself will show him how much he must suffer for the sake of my name" (Acts 9:15-16).

I'm struck every time I read these verses. Steeped, as we all are, in a context where I'm bombarded with marketing and advertising, I expect God to show Paul the grandeur of his legacy as the author of much of the New Testament. I expect God to show Paul how much future scholars will wrestle through the implications of his thought, pour over his letters, and argue over his meanings. I expect God to show Paul a grand vision of all the churches he'll help plant and the transformation of the Roman Empire within a few hundred years. He doesn't. God shows Paul how much he must suffer for the sake of the name of Jesus. No promise of fame, fortune, success, or glory, the call to follow Jesus into his mission and the challenge of suffering go hand in hand. The beauty of grace sustains Paul within the hardships, but following Jesus' call is paramount.

●

Recently Tim, the campus minister who moved to New York City from Rochester, was speaking at the same conference where the first two students he brought had left. By God's grace, Tim has experienced a season of profound fruitfulness in ministry over the past four years. Tim shared wonderful stories about lives transformed, campuses renewed, and world changers being developed, but what stood out to me most was his invitation to follow Jesus into mission. "Friends," he said, "Jesus doesn't promise us that life in mission will be successful or easy. When you enter into life with God, what you get"—he paused here for dramatic effect—"is God, and that is the most beautiful of all."

Two weeks from now our parish will select its next senior pastor, and I'll get a demotion. It's been two years since I felt the weight of responsibility and the call of Jesus to follow him though this transition. Because the Lord is generous, and because of the hard work of many capable leaders, I'll be able to hand off a church that is healthier than I might have imagined two years ago. The joy that accompanies leadership in this phase is not just that the end is in sight, nor the sense of great accomplishment, but the freedom and confidence that comes from Sophia's clear question at lunch that afternoon. Confidence in Jesus' call frees us to follow, it frees us to face the isolating and desolate parts of leadership, it reminds us of the beauty and wonder of God's grace, and it sustains us for a life in mission.

Three years from now the church will not remember this season of struggle. My leadership will be forgotten. But the beauty of

God's grace in the face of Jesus and the call to follow Jesus into mission will be as relevant as ever. May leaders then as now follow Jesus through weighty, lonely, and challenging seasons and discover the beauty of that grace.

For Reflection and Discussion

1. In what ways have you experienced loneliness, betrayal, disappointment, or the weight of responsibility in following Jesus? How did God meet you in this experience?

2. In what ways have you experienced God's radical reorientation in the midst of following him? What have you learned or discovered about God's grace?

3. Many of us do ministry out of a grandiose vision that includes our success or the success of our plans, projects, and communities. How does this chapter challenge this approach?

4. What might it mean to be sustained in ministry by the beauty of God's grace?

10 | Worship

FRIAR Ugo sat back in his chair. "This is all very good," he said.

I'd been describing my experiences of entering into the Scriptures and reflecting on God's invitations in loneliness. I was pleased by the progress and discoveries I'd been making, but something in his affirmation felt not so much disappointed as flat. It was like when I asked a director once how a scene I'd been working on was going, and she said, "It's fine." The understatement pointed to something, but what?

We sat in silence, my face full of questions. His eyes focused not on me but on the small crucifix in the corner of the room. My mind raced. *What had I missed? Does he think I'm making progress? What question should I be asking?*

When I noticed him looking at the crucifix, my internal monologue slowed down a bit. Friar Ugo took a deep breath. "Jason, it's clear to me that you want to love Jesus," he said. "I do!" I said, surprised by his "want to." "Tell me," he continued, "how can you love someone you don't really know?" Now I was offended. Who was this old man to insinuate that I didn't know Jesus? My whole life and ministry was oriented around knowing Jesus, wasn't it?

Friar Ugo seemed to notice my discomfort. "I have no doubt of the sincerity of your commitment to Jesus," he said, "but to know someone is to enter into their story, to grow your compassion and empathy for them and their experience." He paused. "You describe your loneliness and your entering into Scripture as though the point is for Jesus to empathize with you." He was right. I'd loved seeing Jesus' compassion for the marginal in the Gospels. I imagined myself as the woman caught in adultery, the prodigal son, the leper. In Jesus' compassion, I'd felt hopeful. I'd think, *Jesus sees me in my sin, isolation, or fear, and he comes to me in it.* How many times had I told students that Jesus can meet them in their pain, grief, or anger because he entered into pain, grief, anger, even death?

Friar Ugo smiled, "I'm glad for the consolation you feel as you enter into the Scriptures, but I don't think they're the point. What if the loneliness that drives you to seek consolation was meant to expand your heart in compassion for Jesus?" He paused again. "You can't love someone you don't know, and you only know someone whose experience you're willing to enter into with empathy and compassion."

Something clicked. Friar Ugo wasn't denying my faith, my commitment to Jesus, or even the affection for Jesus that energized my spiritual practice. He was inviting me to love Jesus for Jesus' sake, not mine. I suddenly began to see my life with God differently. Years of ministry and Bible study had amassed robust knowledge about Jesus. Years of devotion fueled my commitment to Jesus. But what about friendship with Jesus?

I thought about the song "What a Friend We Have in Jesus." It suddenly struck me how odd the word *friend* is to describe the relationship depicted in the song.

What a friend we have in Jesus,
All our sins and griefs to bear!

What a privilege to carry
Everything to God in prayer!
Oh, what peace we often forfeit,
Oh, what needless pain we bear,
All because we do not carry
Everything to God in prayer!

Imagine a friend to whom you regularly bring grief, sin, burdens, trial, temptations, care, and disappointment, but whose own griefs, trials, temptations, or burdens you never stop to consider. This is the kind of relationship you might have with a therapist, a journal, or confessor, but it's not the love of friendship. This hymn captures something important about the invitation to pray in the midst of difficulties, trials, temptations, and other desolations. This is valuable. But is it friendship?

To grow in friendship with Jesus, Friar Ugo invited me to enter into the Gospels with a fresh perspective, to imagine myself in the scenes as Jesus' friend, one whose concern is for Jesus' well-being. He also invited me to be present to the lingering loneliness that I was feeling and use it as a way of empathizing with Jesus, especially in his times of isolation and loneliness. I didn't know it at the time, but the invitation through these exercises was to a friendship with Jesus that expresses itself not in chummy camaraderie but in worship. Jesus both "came closer" as a friend I could relate to and care for, and "stepped away" as one whose beauty and holiness expanded beyond my neat theological boxes.

Jesus and Peter: Stay Awake

In Jesus's prayer at Gethsemane I'd always imagined Jesus walking away from his disciples, leaving them uncertain about what he was doing and unclear about how painfully distraught he was. But as my eyes were opened I discovered that's not how the passage reads.

Peter, James, and John are with Jesus when he begins to be grieved and agitated. Jesus speaks to them about his desperate need for companionship. Jesus simply wants to be with his friends in the final hours before his passion. Jesus is clearly upset, "grieved, even to death," and his friends promptly fall asleep.

> Jesus went with them to a place called Gethsemane; and he said to his disciples, "Sit here while I go over there and pray." He took with him Peter and the two sons of Zebedee, and began to be grieved and agitated. Then he said to them, "I am deeply grieved, even to death; remain here, and stay awake with me." And going a little farther, he threw himself on the ground and prayed, "My Father, if it is possible, let this cup pass from me; yet not what I want but what you want." Then he came to the disciples and found them sleeping; and he said to Peter, "So, could you not stay awake with me one hour? Stay awake and pray that you may not come into the time of trial; the spirit indeed is willing, but the flesh is weak." Again he went away for the second time and prayed, "My Father, if this cannot pass unless I drink it, your will be done." Again he came and found them sleeping, for their eyes were heavy. So leaving them again, he went away and prayed for the third time, saying the same words. Then he came to the disciples and said to them, "Are you still sleeping and taking your rest? See, the hour is at hand, and the Son of Man is betrayed into the hands of sinners. Get up, let us be going. See, my betrayer is at hand." (Matthew 26:36-46)

The context of this passage makes Peter, James, and John's sleeping even more of a betrayal. Peter had promised, boldly, over dinner, "Though all become deserters because of you, I will never desert you" (Matthew 26:33). Yet, here, a short time after dinner, with no threats or fears for his safety, Peter abandons Jesus to thrash in grief alone on the ground. One time Peter had even chided Jesus, "Do you not care that we are perishing?" (Mark 4:38). He said this because Jesus was asleep in the back of the boat while Peter and the disciples were trying to keep their boat upright in the midst of raging wind and deadly waves. Now, Jesus is the one facing a storm, a storm to darken the sky, mutilate his flesh, and torture him to death, and Peter's asleep.

Justice would spit Peter's words in his face. I'd imagine Jesus coming over to Peter and shaking him awake, "Do you not care that I am perishing?" Jesus' face a mix of sternness and desolation. But Jesus absorbs Peter's injustice and inconsistency. Peter doesn't know it yet, but he's already deserted Jesus.

How could Jesus have been in such obvious distress and his best friends leave him wailing in prayer, in a state of anguish, after being explicitly asked to sit and pray with him? I remembered a scary night in the hospital with Sophia. She came into the emergency room at 4:30 in the afternoon, with chest pain so severe she couldn't breathe. The doctors quickly managed her pain but her underlying condition wasn't diagnosed until 4 a.m. I stood by her bedside or paced in the hallway for those twelve hours. It would have felt wrong to doze off in a chair while she was in such obvious distress. This fact haunted my imagination.

Jesus' response to his friends' sleeping shows dizzying amounts of compassion and self-control. He does not lash out at them in anger and spite, nor does he withdraw from them in bitterness. Jesus reaches out to them, confronting their failure and inviting them again to share in these hours of anguish with him. The contrast between Jesus' desperation and his composed compassion is arresting. How could Jesus, even in the midst of his desperate grief, demonstrate concern for Peter, James, and John?

This pattern happens three times, each one drawing Jesus more deeply into abandonment. He is abandoned by his closest friends even as he abandons himself to the will of God. In evangelical settings I tended to understand the "cup of judgment" Jesus was about to drink as God's just punishment for sin. This is a meaningful doctrine for understanding the mystery of the cross, but it had obscured the relational dynamic here in the text. What if the "cup of judgment" was already pressing on Jesus' lips as his friends left him alone in his moment of need?

Jesus' own scriptural meditation on the cross comes from Psalm 22:6:

> I am a worm, and not human;
>> scorned by others, and despised by the people.

This rejection by his friends must have pained Jesus deeply. Perhaps just as Peter has already abandoned Jesus in his time of need, Jesus' petition for clemency, for the cup to pass by, is already denied. Jesus is alone.

I began to reflect on my experiences of feeling abandoned:

- Mom leaving
- running away
- Mom and Dad dying
- the bitter rejection of friends

I remember staring out the window in more than one empty house on Christmas Day, the physical or emotional distance from home too great to cross. At the time, these experiences felt all-encompassing, but in light of Jesus' experience in the garden, they suddenly seemed small. Sure, there are times I've been over-whelmed with grief or anguish, but I've never been abandoned in my grief by the very friends who promised to sit with me in it. Jesus rightly longed for companionship in these crucial hours, and his friends denied him.

Overfamiliarity with this story kept me from seeing. I'd heard this story every year during Holy Week. As an actor I'd even rehearsed and performed various the adaptations of this scene from *Jesus Christ Superstar* and *Godspell* plenty of times, and yet I'd missed so much. It was as though I were asleep.

I opened my journal. What do I want to say to Jesus?

Jesus, I've been asleep, just like Peter. I'm full of big words about how committed I am to you and to your mission but fail to even notice you in your moment of grief. I'm a terrible friend, drowsy to your needs, consumed by my own desires, dull to your invitations. It breaks my heart to see you waiting alone, and it melts my heart to hear your invitation to watch and pray, especially after failing to really notice you for so long. Is this what it means to grow in compassion for you? I'm curious and want to know more.

Ask the One Who Heard

As I came to the story of Peter's denial (John 18:15-27), my mind and imagination were more alert.

By separating Peter's denial with the story of Jesus' trial before the high priest, John is inviting his readers to use the *outside* (Peter's denial) to interpret the *inside* (Jesus' trial) and vice versa. Overfamiliarity had again clouded my vision. I'd never considered the trial and denial to be intertwined.

Entering the text, I imagined myself watching Peter come into the courtyard, let in by that disciple "known to the high priest" (John 18:15). Peter's there only because his fellow disciple, a man the high priest knows, lets him in. The relational connections carry over into the woman's question at the gate. Of course, she'd ask if he was also a disciple; the one asking for him to be let in was a disciple. Being a disciple of Jesus was not a crime. Even though Jesus was being questioned for his teaching and actions, the act of being his disciple was at best a poor association, not a punishable crime. It would have been natural for Jesus to have some of his disciples come to his trial as witnesses on his behalf. I suddenly tasted bile as the horror of what was unfolding struck me. No one is coming to Jesus' defense.

Jesus' testimony before the high priest opens the floor for testimony. "Ask those who heard what I said," is Jesus' defense (John 18:21). In my mind's eye I see Jesus looking up at Peter and his other disciple. They know what Jesus taught. They were with him night and day. Jesus' words cry out for someone to say, "I heard what Jesus taught; question me." Instead, there is silence and violence.

The scene moves again to Peter. People in the crowd ask him if he was Jesus' disciple. One even asks if he had seen Peter in the garden with Jesus. Peter denies everything.

How is it that every year, when I heard this story, I'd never considered that Peter was in a position to testify on Jesus' behalf? How is it that I'd justified Peter's actions as understandable self-protection? It wasn't. The disciple known to the high priest was in no danger, why should Peter have been? How could both of them have stayed quiet as their friend and rabbi sat in front of them asking for a witness? How could Peter lie in the face of people who recognized him?

Jesus looks at me. "Ask those who heard," he says. I am riveted by his gaze. I've heard Jesus' teaching since I was small. Jesus is speaking directly to me in his moment of need, and my legs are stuck to the ground. I can't speak, paralyzed by shame.

Jesus' gaze continues to pierce my heart, and I begin to imagine his grief. I've never known betrayal like this. Imagine staring into the face of your best friends in your moment of need, knowing that one word could change your suffering, and watch them lie and deny even knowing you. Sure, I've had people lie to and about me, but nothing like that. The depth of Jesus' suffering is so profound. I'd have been crushed by this kind of betrayal. My love, mixed with need, would have rapidly turned to spite and hatred, but Jesus' eyes are not filled with disgust. They are filled with love.

Jesus, everything in me wants you to look away. I can't bear the weight of your gaze. How have I never noticed you before now? How can you possibly bear the weight of this betrayal and still look at me with love? Friar Ugo was right, I don't feel like I know you at all, and yet . . . I don't want to look away. Even as you bear the weight of incalculable betrayal, the sheer beauty of your presence calls to something within me I can't even name.

Behold the Man

Jesus' story continues:

Then Pilate took Jesus and had him flogged. And the soldiers wove a crown of thorns and put it on his head, and they dressed him in a purple robe. They kept coming up to him, saying, "Hail, King of the Jews!" and striking him on the face. Pilate went out again and said to them, "Look, I am bringing him out to you to let you know that I find no case against him." So Jesus came out, wearing the crown of thorns and the purple robe. Pilate said to them, "Here is the man!" When the chief priests and the police saw him, they shouted, "Crucify him! Crucify him!" (John 19:1-6)

Jesus' trial is a mockery of justice. He is brought to Pilate as a would-be messiah, king of the Jews, but there is no evidence presented. Tom Wright comments,

Pilate doesn't understand, and doesn't want to understand, the ins and outs of the odd ways (as they would seem to him) in which the Jews organize their life. But he knows what kings are, what kingdoms are, where they come from, and how they behave. And he knows that it's his job to allow no such thing on his patch. So out he comes with it. "Are you the King of the Jews?"

The idea is, of course, so laughable that he knows, within his own frame of reference, what the answer is. He sees before him a poor man from the wrong part of the country. He has a small band of followers and they've all run away. Of course he's not the king. But . . . maybe he thinks he is. Maybe he's really deluded.

Jesus has not simply been abandoned by his friends, but as his hour has come he is abandoned by his people. Pilate represents the Roman occupation, an enemy of the people of God, a ruthless governor and a pagan. After a fascinating conversation about the nature of power, kingship, authority, and truth, Pilate has him flogged. Jesus' vulnerability has escalated, now he is not only relationally abandoned but also physically beaten. Flogging was a painful but nonlethal way for the Roman government to exercise its power. Roman citizens could not be flogged without a trial and sentence; Jesus has no such citizenship. He is flogged as a public nuisance, an exercise designed to show everyone, including the victim, who's in charge and to discourage any challenge to Roman rule. As a noncitizen Jesus has no court of appeal. He simply must endure the beating.

The symbols of robe and crown are intentionally distorted to increase the abuse. Rather than a crown of laurels, which would have been a symbol of honor and victory, Jesus is given a crown of thorns. The wreath around his head announces failure, dishonor, and shame. Purple cloth was associated with royalty. By dressing Jesus in it they are mocking his claim to kingship. The whole ordeal is designed to symbolically shout to the whole community, "This is what Rome does to your pitiful kings."

As I look at this scene I'm horrified by the violence but also by how easily it is harnessed against someone who simply fits the description. Jesus is clearly no political threat to Pilate or to the Roman occupation. He is beaten anyway. Jesus' protection from imperial violence, if there was to be some, would come from his people who were afforded some liberties and entrusted with their own judicial system. Jesus is offered up by his community instead.

After being bloodied, beaten, and mocked so that Jesus' public humiliation would smash any hope of revolutionary zeal, Pilate brings Jesus out to the crowd. It's a moving scene. Jesus is clearly defeated. His seditious ideas, if there were any, are subverted and crushed. Now Jesus is taken out so that the crowd can tremble before Roman imperial power and beg for mercy on behalf of their bloodied and bruised son. This is how the political game worked. Rome was a bestial regime of total military domination to its enemies but saw itself as benevolent and civilizing to its subjects. All the crowd needed to do was cry out for mercy, humble itself, and Jesus would have been released to them. Even those who disapproved of Jesus could have been comforted to know that he'd been put in his place by Rome.

Instead of mercy, the crowd cries out for his death.

Like the last passage with the outside interpreting the inside and vice versa, this passage is composed similarly. Instead of two layers, there are three. The outermost is Jesus being handed over to Rome, first for examination and then for crucifixion. The second layer is a discussion between Jesus and Pilate about power, authority, and truth. And in the center is Jesus, bloodied and beaten, in a mock robe and thorny crown, standing before the

crowd. This is the focus of John's story. Pilate's words "Behold the   143
man" emphasize the point (John 19:5 NASB).

WORSHIP |

Stopping to behold the man, I'm overwhelmed with emotions. Everything, literally everything that has come before in the Scriptures is standing in front of me. In the face of Jesus is the dignity and authority of human beings made in the image of God with the call to care for the created world. In Jesus' bleeding body is the violence unleashed since Cain murdered his brother. As a captive, Jesus stands in solidarity with his people in Egypt, Assyria, Babylon, Greece, and Rome. In Jesus' testimony before Pilate, he stands in the great prophetic tradition. Jesus' rejection by the temple priests places him in the priestly tradition. Jesus' charge identifies him as king.

I want the crowd to stop. I want to run to Jesus and care for his wounds. I see the political machinations at work. The wheels are turning. I know how this is going to end, and I'm ashamed. "Enough!" I want to say. "Stop, for just a moment, stop and look," but the crowd is shouting, and I'm stuck. My mind flashes to that moment when huddled with my sister and brother under a knitted afghan, listening to the crashing sounds of my parents' dying marriage, I called out to Jesus. The crowd hammers on.

I lift my eyes. A voice in my mind says, "No one takes it [my life] from me, but I lay it down of my own accord. I have power to lay it down, and I have power to take it up again. I have received this command from my Father" (John 10:18). Jesus' absolute freedom steals over me.

Jesus, let me sit here and simply look at you. You have brought the whole story together in one moment. You hold, in your body, the dignity and beauty of human life and all the corruption and vileness of evil. You stare in love, a love freely given, at a crowd screaming for your blood. I could look at you forever like this and never really understand.

The Loneliness of God

"When it was noon, darkness came over the whole land until three in the afternoon. At three o'clock Jesus cried out with a loud voice, 'Eloi, Eloi, lema sabachthani?' which means, 'My God, my God, why have you forsaken me?'" (Mark 15:33-34).

Ronald Rolheiser rightly describes spirituality:

Spirituality is not something on the fringes, an option for those with a particular bent. None of us has a choice. Everyone has to have a spirituality and everyone does have one, either a life-giving one or a destructive one. No one has the luxury of choosing here because all of us are precisely fired into life with a certain madness that comes from the gods and we have to do something with that. We do not wake up in this world calm and serene, having the luxury of choosing to act or not act. We wake up crying, on fire with desire, with madness. What we do with that madness is our spirituality.

Reading these words in the midst of reflection on Jesus made me stop and wonder about Jesus' spirituality. What madness or desire set Jesus' heart ablaze? The Gospel writers present Jesus from four distinct angles, but central to all of them is Jesus' unique identity in relationship with God. The Synoptic Gospels all begin Jesus' ministry with his baptism, where the Spirit descends and the voice of God declares, "You are my Son, the Beloved; with you I am well pleased" (Luke 3:22). John's Gospel reinforces this relationship of intimacy between the Father and Son in his prologue and again early in Jesus' ministry (see John 3:35; 5:20). If Jesus' spirituality, animating passion, and desire swirl around his identity as the beloved Son, what does it mean for Jesus to cry out, "My God, my God, why have you forsaken me?"

This cry of dereliction expresses a negation and abandonment at the very core of Jesus' being. His identity as beloved Son, an identity essential to his self-understanding, is stretched and challenged to the breaking point. In the garden Jesus had abandoned himself to the Father's will. Here, while abandoned by his friends, rejected by his people, and being actively expunged by the empire, Jesus utters the primordial ache of loneliness focused in four words.

As I watch this scene, I'm transfixed by these words, surprised by how much I relate to them. That cry of God-forsakenness was the emotional block around my neck when I couldn't bless Jason Raize. The words describe the restlessness within as I held my daughter. I felt these words in my difficult relationship with my dad and stepbrother. These words capture the sense of abandonment as my prayers bounced off the ceiling and my parents raged overhead. And . . . they are the prayer of Jesus.

My pulse quickened as I remembered my conversation with Friar Ugo. *I do know Jesus*, I thought. These moments of loneliness, of desolation, of isolation enable me to share in Jesus' prayer of abandonment and desolation. What if every lonely moment was an opportunity to enter into the loneliness of God, to learn to love Jesus more deeply by sharing in his suffering? (Might this have been, in part, what Paul meant when he wrote, "I am now rejoicing in my sufferings for your sake, and in my flesh I am completing what is lacking in Christ's afflictions for the sake of his body, that is, the church" [Colossians 1:24]?)

> Jesus, you took on my abandonment so I might take on your belovedness. Every moment of painful estrangement in my life is a mild participation in your desolate prayer. There are no words left. I know you. You know me. It is enough.

For Reflection and Discussion

1. In what ways are you tempted to orient your worship or devotional life in a way that emphasizes God's compassion and empathy with you? What would it mean to reorient worship and devotion in a way that emphasizes your compassion and empathy for Jesus?

2. What stirred in you as you contemplated these passages? How might Jesus be calling you to worship through them?

3. What do you make of the idea that our loneliness is participation in Jesus' loneliness and abandonment? How might the loneliness of God reshape your experience?

4. How might knowing Jesus in his sufferings increase your companionship and intimacy with him? What might this mean for your experience of loneliness?

5. Write a response to this chapter as a note to Jesus.

11 | Witness

THERE'S a passage in *The Life of St. Teresa* describing a dangerous journey. Coming to a river that was overflowing and impossible to cross in a carriage, St. Teresa led the group through the current on foot.

> The current was so strong that she lost her footing, and was on the point of being carried away when our Lord sustained her. "Oh, my Lord!" she exclaimed, with her usual loving familiarity, "when wilt Thou cease from scattering obstacles in our path?" "Do not complain, daughter," the Divine Master answered, "for it is ever thus that I treat My friends." "Ah, Lord, it is also on that account that Thou hast so few!"

Loneliness feels like being wet, cold, and covered in mud. Like Teresa, I want to complain that this is no way to treat a friend. But the question comes back: What if the experience of isolation and loneliness is an invitation to friendship with God in ways that are inaccessible during times when hearts are full?

This book has been a journey into solitude by way of loneliness. Parts may have been uncomfortable to read; some were certainly uncomfortable to write. But I hope you've experienced the patient and persistent call of God to see your loneliness as an opportunity for spiritual growth.

Those who have traveled through seasons of loneliness and discovered solitude, friendship with God, and a deeper sense of God's indwelling presence and transforming power are called to bear witness. Perhaps this is especially true in the church. Our churches are full of people who've prayed sincerely and saw no change, abstained from sex and felt isolated, gave themselves wholeheartedly to ministry and experienced stress, fatigue, isolation, and failure. Without a compassionate witness, the seeds of resentment toward God, the church, and others can grow into a deadly spiritual cancer.

The need for compassionate witness is great outside the church as well. British Prime Minister Theresa May appointed a government minister to work on loneliness after a 2017 study revealed that more than nine million people in Brittan reported feeling lonely always or most often, roughly 13 percent of the total population.

It's no good telling people to be more social. The social bonds that connected us to one another a few generations ago have collapsed or are collapsing. It's no good pretending that technology will bring about a new golden age of connection and well-being. There is an alarmingly high correlation between the distribution curve of the smartphone after 2008 and the increased number of young people who report experiencing social anxiety, loneliness, or social isolation.

We need a compassionate witness!

The gift Friar Ugo gave was his willingness to witness to life with God beyond loneliness.

Friar Ugo knew something about loneliness. For more than forty years he served as a missionary. He loved the people and culture of Angola in a special way. Arriving there as a young missionary he felt as if he had found the place and the people God most wanted him to serve. Shortly after his arrival, however, Angola's political situation deteriorated into civil war. Friar Ugo was forced to leave the country, never to return. As he told the story, I could see the longing in his heart for a home his heart had embraced but never fully enjoyed.

"Love expands the heart and breaks it," Friar Ugo said. "If we are able to grow in compassion for Jesus in his displacement and loneliness, we might discover we have space in our hearts for others too." Ultimately Friar Ugo, and all of us, learn to lean into the promise of friendship with God so that we can live in love and blessing toward the people around us.

As I sat with Friar Ugo, I felt like a recipient of his expanded heart. He listened. As he invited me into a spiritual journey, he simultaneously bore witness to a life with God that was richer than I'd known before.

If we let it, an invitation from God in the midst of the loneliness can be transformed into a meaningful witness. For example, in an age of geographic and cultural displacement, there is an urgent call for the people of God to lead the way in welcoming refugees, offering hospitality to strangers, reuniting families, and caring for the homeless. There is a holy moment in the weekly worship service at All Angels' Church in Manhattan, a little piece of sung liturgy that marks the transition from Scripture and prayer to the Eucharist. The words, composed by a former parishioner, Ron Melrose, sail above the congregation:

Come to the table, come to the feast.
All are invited, greatest to least.
Sins have been pardoned, divisions have ceased.
Come to the table, come to the feast.
Come to the feast.

As these words are sung by a community of women and men from vastly different backgrounds, street homeless to finance professionals, a strange holiness—earthy, pungent, and profound—settles over the congregation. For the next few moments we glimpse what it means to be the family of God. This is a community that knows what it's like to be displaced. Meeting God in loneliness and vulnerability is reshaping us. As we gather around the Lord's Table we're physically reminded of God's call to love across difference. We witness to the liberating and humanizing work of Jesus, even as we fumble to figure out how to be a community together.

What would it look like if those of us who've had our hearts broken by loneliness discovered, through friendship with God in solitude, the space to listen empathetically to others? What might it mean for us to take an interest in the well-being of those who are displaced because of war, migration, incarceration, unemployment, illness, or homelessness? How might God transform us from loneliness to solitude to a witnessing community?

Being a Witness

One of the gifts this journey through loneliness can give is that it strips away the successes, identities, and social expectations that shape so much of our lives. Like Moses and Hagar, we can be driven into the desert by failure or by injustice and discover the God who sees and hears. We return from that encounter with a compelling testimony about who God is and what God has done.

There is something arresting about a woman or man who's been transformed by an encounter with God in the desert. When Jesus returned from his time in the desert, he immediately began to draw crowds who flocked to his teaching. Those who have met God in the desert are called to witness to the God they've encountered.

From 2004 to 2008 there was a profound movement of God at Columbia University in New York City. Students began to come to faith regularly. The core curriculum, a mandatory class for all Columbia students that inducts freshmen into a secular humanist worldview, was being winsomely challenged by a small group of students. There were reports of miracles. Students reported freedom from dark moods, depression, anxiety, and addictions. The Christian community, which used to meet in an obscure room away from the main campus, was suddenly at the center of campus life, mediating crucial conversations.

As area ministry director for InterVarsity's ministry in New York City, I was delighted and curious about all that God was doing. Two names kept coming up in the story students were telling, Jonathan and Gabby. These students were at the center of what God was doing, and I wanted to understand more. Fascinatingly, both Jonathan and Gabby had experienced God in the desert. Gabby grew up in a context where her housing wasn't secure. An immigrant, exposed to the vulnerabilities that come without solid access to housing, Gabby encountered the God who sees. Jonathan grew up in rural poverty. Home was physically secure but emotionally turbulent. As a young man Jonathan had already experienced exposure and vulnerability beyond his years. He met God in the wilderness of his need and exposure. As Jonathan and Gabby gave themselves first to friendship with God and then to ministry on campus, they modeled a kind of freedom irresistible to students around them. Why worry about your GPA going down, when God has taken you from the street to an elite university? If God has carried you from physical and emotional desperation to the corridors of cultural influence, why not trust that God can provide for you in the midst of it? It was Gabby and Jonathan's humility, the conviction that they and the campus were loved by God, and freedom from the worries and anxieties that dominate student life in elite universities that gave credibility to their witness to Jesus. This was credibility formed in the desert.

Part of what made the witness of Jonathan, Gabby, and the other Columbia students so compelling was that it spoke to the anxiety and ambition too common in elite universities. You would think that young people at the world's most prestigious universities would rest assured, confident in the opportunity structures that support their learning. Too often the opposite is true. Imposter syndrome, stress, anxiety, depression, and fierce competition can characterize the student experience. As was true of Jacob, there is a grasping ambition within all of us that turns potential collaborators to rivals, successes to status markers, and blessing into toil.

A beautiful hymn from the early church celebrates relinquishing our grasping in light of all Jesus is and accomplished.

Let the same mind be in you that was in Christ Jesus,

> who, though he was in the form of God,
>> did not regard equality with God
>> as something to be exploited,
> but emptied himself,
>> taking the form of a slave,
>> being born in human likeness.
> And being found in human form,
>> he humbled himself
>> and became obedient to the point of death—
>> even death on a cross.
> Therefore God also highly exalted him
>> and gave him the name
>> that is above every name,

so that at the name of Jesus

    every knee should bend,

    in heaven and on earth and under the earth,

and every tongue should confess

    that Jesus Christ is Lord,

    to the glory of God the Father. (Philippians 2:5-11)

This is the song of a people who have learned to grasp onto and wrestle with the God who is self-giving to the core. If Jesus let go of equality with God all the way to the cross for us, surely we can learn to live in generosity and trust. In an age of scarcity, anxiety, and fierce competition, we need this kind of witness.

Listening and Seeing

Perhaps one of the most profound ways to witness is to listen well and deeply. A friend who teaches relationships skills is fond of saying, "Listening to someone well feels so much like loving them that most can't tell the difference." Our existential loneliness is, at its core, loneliness for God. Listening to our restlessness, to our desire, and for the presence of God is a way of attending to God's love.

Those of us who have heard God's still, small voice are called to help others hear it as well. Recently, I was with Joe, a friend who is also a spiritual director. "Did you notice, the way your daughter asked for you to share more of your thoughts and feelings with her this week?" He asked. "Sure," I said, not knowing where he was going. "Well, it seems like you've been wanting to grow in your awareness of God's love for you," he said, "perhaps, listening to your daughter and sharing with her is the context in which God is wanting to communicate love to you." Of course, it was. Why didn't I see that?

In an age of accelerated technology and increased distraction, the simple act of listening to ourselves, to others, and to God is a powerful witness. Remember the last time someone listened attentively to you while you shared something important? Remember how it felt? What if the church became a place of deep, empathic listening?

Over the last ten years there has been an increasing interest in spiritual direction among evangelicals. Brother Bede, a Benedictine monk in the Order of the Holy Cross, said to me recently, "Our guest house used to be filled with small parish retreats. These days, we're full of people from evangelical churches who want spiritual direction."

In his book *Them: Why We Hate Each Other and How to Heal*, Republican senator Ben Sasse laments the erosion of the "tribes" that connect us to one another by virtue of place, family, neighborhood connections, deep friendships, worshiping communities, meaningful work associations, and the increase of "anti-tribes," communities mediated by technology, experienced individually, and organized by shared dislikes. According to Sasse, the end result of this is not just increased contentiousness, spite, and disillusionment in the public square but also a dramatic spike in loneliness. Sasse writes, "Suddenly, all of America feels marginalized and ignored. We're all standing there in the dark, feeling powerless and isolated, pleading: 'Don't you see me?'"

Sasse's language is fascinating. There is something visceral about our need to be and feel seen. Perhaps what makes social media likes and hearts so addictive is that they trigger a sense of being noticed. Perhaps the longing for spiritual direction is, at heart, a longing to be seen, to be heard, to be noticed. If we cultivate a capacity to listen well, many will benefit from our witness.

Listening well is especially powerful when we're confronted with grief or loss. When our goldfish died our then-seven-year-old daughter sobbed uncontrollably. We celebrated and eulogized

his life and buried him among our plants. That afternoon our
daughter made markers for his grave, working out her feelings in
a variety of words, actions, and processes. We kept the memorial
up for several weeks until it faded into the background of our
daily rhythms. When we finally cleaned up the memorial, the
grief had transformed into a sense of appreciation and acceptance.
Completely by accident it was probably the healthiest grieving
I've ever witnessed.

The death of a pet goldfish is a small bereavement. The death
of a parent, spouse, sister, brother, friend, dream, ability, or season
is much deeper. The isolation that comes in waves shakes us to
our core.

Many of us live by a cultural commandment to "move on."
Rather than accept the vulnerability of grief, submitting to its
rhythms, we're in a hurry to get back to normal. But what is
normal after your brother dies? What's *normal* when a dream
you've been chasing for a decade collapses around you? What's
normal when you watch your mom succumb to cancer a week
before you give birth to her first grandson?

Paul wrote in Romans, "We also boast in our sufferings,
knowing that suffering produces endurance, and endurance produces character, and character produces hope, and hope does not
disappoint us, because God's love has been poured into our hearts
through the Holy Spirit that has been given to us" (Romans 5:3-5).
Hope, in this passage, is inextricably connected to witness. Paul
is not denying the severity of suffering. He is bearing witness to
God's grace in Jesus in the midst of it. When we listen well, seeing
and hearing the people around us, we communicate the love of
God and the hope of life with him.

Those of us who have walked through the valley of the shadow
of death, who've sat with Jesus while it felt as if our insides were
being ripped apart, can offer hope to others who are grieving.

I'm grateful to Jimmy, John, Francis, Ben, and Jeff, who showed up months after my dad died, after the ceremonial grieving was done but the actual grief had only started. Jimmy asked the same three questions about grieving my dad three months in a row and listened to me without judgment or boredom. John moved an incredibly full schedule to make a morning coffee. Ben initiated on the one-year anniversary of Dad's death and again a few months later. These friends witnessed to the hope of the gospel by simple presence.

Speaking and Risk

The call to witness always comes with a risk of rejection. In my first week as a campus minister in New York City I heard several potentially isolating comments. "Just don't try to convert us," a fellow campus minister from another religion chided as she walked out the door. "Wait, you're a missionary? How disgusting!" Jed said, and began to list the failures and injustices of Christian missionaries. These comments, and many others, were designed to create shame. Being one of "those kinds of Christians," the kind who seek to persuade others of the truth and beauty of the gospel, is shamed as wrong, bad, oppressive, self-serving, judgmental, intolerant, or worse.

A commitment to sharing faith can feel countercultural and potentially isolating, but those who, in isolation, have discovered life with God can embrace the call to witness. St. Dominic, a contemporary of St. Francis, once said that he wanted only to speak to God or about God. He was said to always have a joyful countenance despite that he preached in communities so hostile that his life was regularly threatened. One day a group of Cathars promised to kill him if he traveled from one village to the next. Dominic's friends suggested sneaking him out of town. Dominic insisted on traveling to the next village, singing loudly the whole way so anyone who wanted to find him would be able to.

The evangelist, activist, or witness is invited to embrace risk for the sake of others. Like Esther, God has placed us in contexts that require words, actions, noncompliance, and even sometimes martyrdom. When Jesus said, "Blessed are you when people revile you and persecute you and utter all kinds of evil against you falsely on my account. Rejoice and be glad, for your reward is great in heaven, for in the same way they persecuted the prophets who were before you" (Matthew 5:11-12), he clearly understood both the risk and reward of faithfully representing God's character in this way. In the Old Testament, prophets were generally not people of high social status or wealth. They were blessed not because their lives were easy, safe, or comfortable, but because they knew God and called others to return to his covenant faithfulness.

Still, each time we speak, our words can be misunderstood. The effort to share our story may be met with resistance, rejection, or cool indifference.

Here's a story from the desert fathers about the leader Abba John the Dwarf.

> One day when he was sitting in front of the church, the brethren were consulting him about their thoughts. One of the old men who saw it became a prey to jealousy and said to him, "John, your vessel is full of poison." Abba John said to him, "That is very true, Abba; and you have said that when you only see the outside, but if you were able to see the inside, too, what would you say then?"

Notice the way Abba John doesn't become defensive, dejected, or despondent. Usually when I'm called terrible names, my first instinct is to fight back. I assume the person doesn't understand my motives, intentions, history, or experience. I can turn inward and brood over the hurtful remark. But in those moments when I'm full of God's grace, rejoicing in the gospel, and open to God's work, I can respond differently.

Abba John assumes that criticism and rejection, even criticism and rejection coming from impure motives, bring an opportunity for deeper transformation by God's grace. He accepts the criticism and laments his need for deeper transformation.

What would it be like if those of us following Jesus into mission were so steeped in the grace of God that we could receive criticism without defensiveness, endure painful rejection without despondency, and receive even disappointments as a gift of grace? That kind of witness would be a powerful apologetic for the gospel.

Jesus' Witness

The invitations God gives us in loneliness, in Scripture, bring us to Jesus who says, "Wait with me." Jesus embraced loneliness and isolation deeper and more profoundly than we know. He embraced the call to leave an eternal home of intimacy, sufficiency, and potency to become helpless, vulnerable, killable. Jesus was driven into the desert, where he became famished with hunger before being tempted by the accuser himself. Jesus regularly resisted the urge to grasp after power, privilege, or prestige, choosing instead to cling to God's word and will, even to death. Jesus' teaching revealed a profound attentiveness. His parables, sayings, and actions regularly call out for those who have ears to listen deeply. Jesus grieved deeply, not only at the death of his friend but also at the hardness of heart he encountered in Jerusalem. Unlike Esther, who rightly feared that her taking risk for others *could* lead to her death, Jesus embraced a mission that *would* certainly lead to his death. Jesus' compassion, teaching, and healing ministry were anchored in a deep awareness of what God was doing. Jesus' commitment to follow God's will led him to total abandonment, utter rejection, torture, and death.

I used to think that Jesus' isolation, misunderstanding, rejection, and loneliness would mean that Jesus could sympathize with me in my loneliness. I now believe that my experiences of loneliness and isolation help me to know Jesus. At the center of the Christian story is God, in Jesus, utterly rejected, isolated, alone. The One who created us for relationship out of love endured the worst kind of obliteration we could invent. Stretching flesh between earth and sky, the lonely, isolated, abandoned One cries out words of mercy (Luke 23:34), inviting us, even in anguish, to wait with him so we might grow in friendship with God.

It is through this loneliness of God that we're invited to know and love him. It's through this strange participation in the loneliness of God that we're summoned to love others. To be human is to be lonely. These days loneliness, depression, and anxiety are accelerating. We're desperate to reconnect. We're desperate for transformation.

What would happen if we met God in the midst of our isolation, loneliness, grief, and vulnerability? What if our loneliness became the context for a deeper life with God and greater compassion for others?

I pray that these pages have inspired you to explore the Scriptures afresh for God's transforming work in the midst of loneliness. More than that, I pray you will discover that the loneliness, isolation, and disorientation you've experienced leads you to know Jesus, to wait with him, empathize with him, to become his friend. And I pray that you might become a witness to a lonely world of the beauty and wonder of the One who endured the worst possible loneliness so you would never be alone.

For Reflection and Discussion

1. How have you met God in these chapters? What insights, perspectives, feelings, or thoughts are most significant?

2. How might Jesus be inviting you to witness to his work in your life?

3. Who do you know that may be experiencing isolation or loneliness in this season? How might God be inviting you to be present to and demonstrate love to them?

4. What next steps would you like to take in your life with God?

Acknowledgments

THIS book is the fruit of more than a decade-long friendship that doesn't appear in its pages. Greg Jao saw my desire to write and chose to believe that this desire was a gift to steward rather than a distraction to manage. Greg chose to believe this long before there was evidence to support it. It was through Greg's invitation to a prospective authors' consultation that the ideas for this book came into a viable form. Thank you, Greg! Your leadership inspires me.

I'm deeply grateful for Cindy Bunch, associate publisher and director of editorial at IVP, for walking alongside me through this project from big idea to its current form. Your patience, perspective, and persistence have been a real gift. Thank you for making this whole process a joy.

Special thanks to Tom Hansen, who took over my leadership responsibilities during fall 2018 so I could write. This book couldn't have happened without you.

I'm grateful for Jonathan Walton, Noemi Vega, Tim Craig, and the many others whose stories help give color to this book. Thank you for trusting me with your words.

This book would not have been possible without Fr. Ugo, whose insight into loneliness set me on a journey of discovery. I thank God for your ministry.

ACKNOWLEDGMENTS |

Within the community of women and men whose presence and spiritual friendship have made this book possible, I'm especially grateful for Jimmy Lee, who regularly asked about the book's progress. Francis Hsueh and Jeff Mays do not cease to inspire me with their writing and creativity. Your belief in this project means a lot. The community of All Angels' Church in Manhattan has blessed many writers over the years. Thank you for your involvement and support. I'm also deeply grateful for the Anglican Order of Preachers, whose way of life has sustained this project.

To mama, whose generosity and selflessness blesses people around the corner and around the globe. Thank you for the many ways you are a gift to our family.

To my daughters, thank you for listening to chapters and offering fresh perspective. Malaya, your appreciations energized and encouraged me. Serena, your questions and candid feedback, especially when there was something confusing or vague, were spot-on.

Sophia, thank you for the hours of writing you made possible. You fill our home and our ministry with life, creativity, energy, and focus we wouldn't otherwise have. Thank you for the many times you've gotten me unstuck in writing and in life. Mahal kita!

Notes

1. See

1   *To be human is to be lonely*: This chapter is an expanded version of Jason Gaboury, "Just Tell Me What I Need to Know: Loneliness After College," InterVarsity, July 22, 2016, https://intervarsity.org/blog/just-tell-me -what-i-need-know-loneliness-after-college.

3   *It turns out that the people who reported*: Katherine Hobson, "Feeling Lonely? Too Much Time on Social Media May Be Why?" *NPR*, March 6, 2017, www.npr.org/sections/health-shots/2017/03/06/518362255/feeling -lonely-too-much-time-on-social-media-may-be-why.

     Americans are right that the bonds: Robert Putnam, *Bowling Alone* (New York: Simon & Schuster, 2000), 402.

4   *The English term* very *is a weak translation*: Francis Brown, Samuel R. Driver, and Charles A. Briggs, *Enhanced Brown-Driver-Briggs Hebrew and English Lexicon* (Oxford: Clarendon Press, 1977), 547.

12   *Your desire for more of God*: Ruth Haley Barton, *Sacred Rhythms* (Downers Grove, IL: InterVarsity Press, 2006), 24.

2. Leave

14   *In total, therefore, about 1 billion persons*: "Migration and Human Mobility," UN Department of Economic and Social Affairs, May 2012, www.un.org /millenniumgoals/pdf/Think Pieces/13_migration.pdf.

     The teenagers at our church: Jean Carlos Arce, "Reading Scripture with Immigrant Youth: Let the Children Come to Me," Fuller Youth Institute, August 30, 2018, https://fulleryouthinstitute.org/blog/scripture-and -immigrant-youth?.

21   *If we feel a disorder in our attachment*: Patti Clement, "What is Your Basic Hunger and Thirst This Lent," *Patti Clement* (blog), March 6, 2013, https://patticlement.wordpress.com/2013/03/06/what-is-your-basic -hunger-and-thirst-this-lent.

3. Desert

27   *Anxiety as failure in advance*: Seth Godin, "Anxiety Is Nothing," *Seth's Blog*, March 18, 2010, https://seths.blog/2010/03/anxiety-is-nothing-but -repeatedly-experiencing-failure-in-advance.

     Over the last decade, anxiety has overtaken depression: Benoit Denizet-Lewis, "Why Are More American Teenagers Than Ever Suffering from

Severe Anxiety?" *New York Times*, October 11, 2017, www.nytimes
.com/2017/10/11/magazine/why-are-more-american-teenagers-than
-ever-suffering-from-severe-anxiety.html.

28 *The God of Sinai is one who thrives*: Belden Lane, *The Solace of Fierce
Landscapes* (New York: Oxford University Press, 1998), 43.

30 *"Sarah's reaction to the plan"*: Catherine Clark Kroeger and Mary J. Evans,
The IVP Women's Bible Commentary (Downers Grove, IL: InterVarsity
Press, 2002), 10.

    "The story would end here": Kroeger and Evans, *IVP Women's Bible
Commentary*, 11.

32 *"Documents from ancient Mesopotamia"*: Kroeger and Evans, *IVP Women's
Bible Commentary*, 11.

33 *"Patricia was sold to a local gang"*: "Patricia's Story," *Restore*, April 23, 2018,
https://restorenyc.org/updates/patricias-story.

36 *"The sixteenth-century Spanish Carmelite reformer"*: Belden Lane, *The
Solace of Fierce Landscapes* (New York: Oxford University Press, 1998), 73.

39 *"When Abba Macarius was returning from the marsh"*: Abba Macarius 11,
"Life and Sayings of Holy Abba Makarios the Great of Egypt," *Mystagogy
(blog)*, Friday, January 19, 2018, www.johnsanidopoulos.com/2018/01
/life-and-sayings-of-holy-abba-makarios.html

    "Freedom's just another word for nothing left to lose": Janis Joplin, "Me and
Bobby McGee," *Pearl*, Columbia, 1971. The song was written by Kris
Kristofferson and Fred Foster in 1969.

4. Grasp

41 *I felt the worst at the exact moment*: Jason Duff, "The Mental Shift People
Make in Their Twenties," *Inc.*, July 7, 2016, www.inc.com/empact/the
-mental-shift-ambitious-people-make-in-their-20s.html.

46 *He blessed Esau with the gifts*: Jonathan Sacks, "Was Jacob Right to Take
the Blessings?" *Chabad.org*, accessed October 7, 2019, www.chabad.org
/parshah/article_cdo/aid/2757118/jewish/Was-Jacob-Right-to-Take-the
-Blessings.htm.

55 Lion King *lyrics*: Lebo M., Hans Zimmer, Julie Taymor, and Jay Rifkin,
"Endless Night," track 16 on *Disney Presents The Lion King: Original
Broadway Cast Recording*, Walt Disney Records, 1997.

5. Listen

57 *Our hearts and minds are so fashioned*: Ronald Rolheiser, *The Restless
Heart* (New York: Image Books, Doubleday, 2004), 48-49.

58 *Every ping, ding and vibration is designed*: Michael Enright, "The Sunday Edition with Michael Enright," *CBCListen*, September 14, 2018, www.cbc .ca/listen/live-radio/1-57-the-sunday-edition/clip/15597763-you-cant -stop-checking-your-phone-because-silicon-valley-designed-it-that-way.

59 *pushed to the edge of loneliness*: Douglas Coupland, *Life After God* (New York: Simon & Shuster, 1994), 222.

  Now—here is my secret: Coupland, *Life After God*, 365.

61 *games and amusements of mankind*: Henry David Thoreau, *Walden* (New York: Houghton Mifflin, 1854), 9-10.

  A fiercely Yahwist prophet: Beth Glazier-McDonald, "Elijah," in *Eerdmans Dictionary of the Bible, ed.* D. N. Freedman, A. C. Myers, and A. B. Beck (Grand Rapids: Eerdmans, 2000), 395.

63 *Whenever I found myself up against my mother's*: Trevor Noah, *Born a Crime* (London: John Murray, 2016), 9-10.

64 *how insane the week had been*: Noah, *Born a Crime*, afterword.

69 *Listen carefully, my child*: Joan Chittister, *The Rule of Benedict: A Spirituality for the 21st Century* (New York: Crossroad, 2010), 3.

  Benedictine spirituality forms us to listen: Chittister, *Rule of Benedict*, 74-75.

75 *Religion is the sigh of the oppressed creature*: Karl Marx, *A Contribution to the Critique of Hegel's Philosophy of Right* (Paris: Deutsch-Französische Jahrbücher, 1843), 7, 10.

  David Kinnaman's research: David Kinnaman, *You Lost Me: Why Young Christians Are Leaving Church and Rethinking Faith* (Grand Rapids: Baker, 2011), 19.

76 *On the outside, always looking in*: Benji Pasek and Justin Paul, "Waving Through a Window," *Dear Evan Hansen*, 2015.

  What if everyone knew?: Benji Pasek and Justin Paul, "Words Fail," *Dear Evan Hansen*, 2015.

7. Risk

85 *I am an Ivy League educated black male*: Jonathan Walton, "Racism Is Ruining My Marriage," *HuffPost*, March 17, 2015, www.huffpost.com /entry/racism-is-ruining-my-marriage_b_6871724.

86 *Loneliness rarely travels alone*: John T. Cacioppo and William Patrick, *Loneliness: Human Nature and the Need for Social Connection* (New York: W. W. Norton, 2008), 83.

87   *According to Pew research 53 percent*: Monica Anderson, Skye Toor, Lee Rainie, and Aaron Smith, "Activism in Social Media," Pew Research Center, July 11, 2018, www.pewinternet.org/2018/07/11/public-attitudes -toward-political-engagement-on-social-media.

The internet was born into a world: Johann Hari, *Lost Connections* (New York: Bloomsbury, 2018), 88.

88   *When even our babies are a target market*: Marilyn McEntyre, *Word by Word: A Daily Spiritual Practice* (Grand Rapids: Eerdmans, 2016), 96.

90   *Esther finds its meaning*: Debra Reid, *Esther*, Tyndale Old Testament Commentaries 13 (Downers Grove, IL: InterVarsity Press, 2008), 24.

91   *Confronted by sexism like that of Xerxes*: John Goldingay, *Ezra, Nehemiah, and Esther for Everyone* (Louisville, KY: Westminster John Knox Press, 2012), 160.

92   *Imagine turning the process of selecting a spouse*: John Ortberg, "Overcoming Your Shadow Mission: Esther," *Vimeo*, June 27, 2016, https:// vimeo.com/172367616.

93   *The king's beauty contest is pathetic*: Goldingay, *Ezra, Nehemiah, and Esther*, 163.

94   *The word translated "favor"*: Reid, *Esther*, 80.

Esther has assumed Vashti's crown: Reid, *Esther*, 83.

95   *If in the first act you have a pistol*: Donald Rayfield, *Anton Chekhov: A Life* (New York: Henry Holt, 1997), 203.

98   *He was not who we were waiting for*: Jonathan Walton, *Twelve Lies that Hold America Captive and the Truth That Can Set Us Free* (Downers Grove, IL: InterVarsity Press, 2018), 183.

99   *Since that day many men said to us*: Sheldon Harnick, "When Messiah Comes," *Fiddler on the Roof*, 1964.

100 *The oppressive, corrosive, divisive system of racism*: Walton, "Racism Is Ruining My Marriage."

8. Ponder

102 *We can now create machines*: B. J. Fogg, quoted in Richard Freed, "The Tech Industry's War on Kids," *Medium*, March 12, 2018, https://medium .com/@richardnfreed/the-tech-industrys-psychological-war-on-kids -c452870464ce. Persuasive technology, also called persuasive design, is the science of applying psychological and sociological research to consumer technology in an effort to influence, direct, and change human behavior.

106 *Such a son is an answer to the prayers*: Michael Wilcock, *The Savior of the World: The Message of Luke's Gospel* (Downers Grove, IL: InterVarsity Press, 1979), 33-34.

108 *Definition of* dialogizomai: James A. Swanson, *Dictionary of Biblical Languages with Semantic Domains: Greek (New Testament)* (Oak Harbor, WA: Logos Research Systems, 1997).

110 *St. Francis's first Nativity*: Gretchen Filz, "The Story of St. Francis of Assisi and the First Nativity Scene, as told by St. Bonaventure," *Catholic Company*, December 21, 2016, www.catholiccompany.com/getfed/story -francis-assisi-first-navity-scene-5955.

    Tradition has them knocking at an inn door: N. T. Wright, *Luke for Everyone* (London: SPCK, 2004), 21.

111 *Greek term translated "ponder"*: Swanson, *Dictionary of Biblical Languages.*

    Compassion begins with: Ronald Rolheiser, "A Culture of Amazement," *RonRolheiser, OMI* (blog), August 19, 2001, http://ronrolheiser.com /a-culture-of-amazement/#.XZ4VymZ7nIV.

116 *The nature of water is soft*: Poemen, quoted in Benedicta Ward, *The Sayings of the Desert Fathers*, rev. ed. (Collegeville, MN: Liturgical Press, 1984), 162.

10. Worship

133 *What a friend we have in Jesus*: Joseph Scriven, "What a Friend We Have in Jesus," 1855.

141 *Pilate doesn't understand*: N. T. Wright, *John for Everyone, part 2, Chapters 11-21* (London: SPCK, 2004), 114.

144 *Spirituality is not something on the fringes*: Ronald Rolheiser, *The Holy Longing: The Search for a Christian Spirituality* (New York: Doubleday, 1999), 6.

11. Witness

147 *The current was so strong*: Teresa of Ávila, *The Life of Saint Teresa of Ávila by Herself* (Boston: Digireads, 2009), 548.

148 *Nine million people in Britain feel lonely*: Ceylan Yeginsu, "U.K. Appoints a Minister for Loneliness," *New York Times*, January 17, 2018, www.nytimes .com/2018/01/17/world/europe/uk-britain-loneliness.html.

149 *Come to the table*: Ronald Melrose, "Doxology / Come to the Feast," 1992.

154 *America feels marginalized*: Ben Sasse, *Them: Why We Hate Each Other and How to Heal* (New York: St. Martin's Press, 2016), 9.

157 *Leader Abba John the Dwarf*: "Abba John the Dwarf," Patristics Project, accessed October 10, 2019, www.patristics.co/sayings.

formatio

TRADITION. EXPERIENCE.
TRANSFORMATION.

Formatio books from InterVarsity Press follow the rich tradition of the church in the journey of spiritual formation. These books are not merely about being informed, but about being transformed by Christ and conformed to his image. Formatio stands in InterVarsity Press's evangelical publishing tradition by integrating God's Word with spiritual practice and by prompting readers to move from inward change to outward witness. InterVarsity Press uses the chambered nautilus for Formatio, a symbol of spiritual formation because of its continual spiral journey outward as it moves from its center. We believe that each of us is made with a deep desire to be in God's presence. Formatio books help us to fulfill our deepest desires and to become our true selves in light of God's grace.